Lynn Pardie, PhD
Tracy Luchetta, PhD
Editors

The Construction of Attitudes Toward Lesbians and Gay Men

Pre-publication
REVIEWS,
COMMENTARIES,
EVALUATIONS . . .

"**H**eterosexism and homonegative attitudes are analyzed from psychological, sociocultural, and institutional perspectives. The specific contributions include examination of homophobia in academia, the role of legal ideology in constructing attitudes, internalized homophobia in the context of therapeutic process, and the role of spiritual development in transcending heterosexism. Readers will gain an understanding of the intricate relationship between psychological and cultural heterosexism. Of particular interest, the contributors draw on their analyses to suggest strategies that can combat the pervasive heterosexism in American culture."

Henry L. Minton, PhD
Professor,
University of Windsor,
Ontario, Canada

"**T**he chapters in this volume examine attitudes of heterosexuals toward lesbians and gay men, but they also examine the attitudes of lesbian and gay people toward their sexuality and toward themselves. The authors make useful connections between social attitudes and institutional norms, political rhetoric, and therapeutic practices. Within these chapters, readers will find valuable citations to literature on the social and personal origins of homophobia and heterosexism, as well as timely suggestions for confronting these social problems."

Cynthia Burack, PhD
Assistant Professor,
Department of Political Science
and Center for Women's Studies
and Gender Research,
University of Florida,
Gainesville

"**T**aken together, the diverse chapters in this book focus our attention not just on how individuals construct negative attitudes toward lesbians and gay men, but also on how such constructions are sustained—and by implication, how they may be changed and ultimately dismantled.

From an examination of the relationships between negative attitudes toward gay men and lesbians and the stigma of HIV/AIDS, to the roles of the law and an individual's spiritual development in continuing the stigmatization of non-heterosexual identities, the reader will learn important strategies for understanding, addressing, and confronting individual and cultural heterosexism.

The interdisciplinary nature of this book offers a diversity of tools for combating heterosexism. Practitioners of therapy are offered a sensitive means for integrating an understanding of internalized ho-mophobia into therapeutic practice, while developmental psychologists and sociologists are offered a way of understanding negative attitudes toward gay men and lesbians as a reflection of individual and cultural developmental, psychological, and spiritual limitations. Those engaged in political activism are treated to a powerful analysis of the impact and potential of various approaches to fighting heterosexism through/with the law. The reader is likely to come away from reading this book with a deeper commitment and a greater ability to understand and confront heterosexism in specific, practical, and effective ways."

Jacqueline S. Weinstock, PhD
Assistant Professor,
Human Development and Family
Studies Program,
University of Vermont,
Burlington

Harrington Park Press
An Imprint of The Haworth Press, Inc.

The Construction
of Attitudes Toward
Lesbians and Gay Men

HAWORTH Gay & Lesbian Studies
John P. De Cecco, PhD
Editor in Chief

The Construction of Attitudes Toward Lesbians and Gay Men

Lynn Pardie, PhD
Tracy Luchetta, PhD
Editors

Harrington Park Press
An Imprint of The Haworth Press, Inc.
New York • London • Oxford

Published by

Harrington Park Press, an imprint of The Haworth Press, Inc., 10 Alice Street, Binghamton, NY 13904-1580

Cover design by Marylouise E. Doyle.

The Library of Congress has cataloged the hardcover edition of this book as:

The construction of attitudes toward lesbians and gay men / Lynn Pardie, Tracy Luchetta, editors.
    p. cm.
    Includes bibliographical references and index.
    ISBN 0-7890-0590-5 (alk. paper)
    1. Lesbians—United States—Public opinion. 2. Gay men—United States—Public opinion. 3. Homosexuality—United States—Public opinion. 4. Homophobia—United States. 5. Public opinion—United States. I. Pardie, Lynn. II. Luchetta, Tracy.
HQ75.6.U5C654   1999
306.76′6—dc21   99-14374
                                                        CIP

ISBN 1-56023-942-5 (pbk.)

CONTENTS

ABOUT THE EDITORS

Lynn Pardie, PhD, is a clinical psychologist and Associate Professor of Psychology at the University of Illinois at Springfield, where she teaches courses on psychological assessment, personality, psychological aspects of diversity, and transpersonal psychology. Dr. Pardie's professional interests currently include identity development and relationship issues for lesbians and gay men, and the intersection of psychology and spirituality.

Tracy Luchetta, PhD, is currently Associate Professor of Psychology and Women's Studies at the University of Wisconsin—Green Bay, where she teaches courses on the psychology of women and abnormal psychology. Dr. Luchetta's research interests include lesbian and gay studies, depression, and personal wellness as political resistance.

Contributors

Francis Carleton, PhD, is Associate Professor of Social Change and Development and Women's Studies at the University of Wisconsin at Green Bay. He has published a series of articles that explore how to use an ethic of care to critically analyze affirmative action and sex discrimination jurisprudence.

Linda Gannon, PhD, is Professor of Psychology at Southern Illinois University at Carbondale and a licensed clinical psychologist. Her most recent publication is *Women and Aging: Transcending the Myths* (1999), Routledge.

Elizabeth Johnson, PhD, is a licensed psychologist in private practice in Appleton, Wisconsin. She is the author (with A. J. Schwartz) of "Returning Students," in P. A. Grayson and K. Cauley (Eds.), *College Psychotherapy* (1989), published by Guilford Press.

Preface

This book developed out of work prepared for a symposium conducted at the 1996 Meeting of the Society for Community Research and Action, in Chicago, Illinois. Interest in the symposium and the book evolved out of shared concern regarding the need for positive transformation, at cultural and individual levels, in attitudes toward same-sex erotic relationships.

More than twenty years have elapsed since the American Psychological Association officially passed a resolution proactively supporting the destigmatization of particular sexual orientations. Similar positions had already been taken by various other professional organizations, including the American Sociological Association, the National Association for Mental Health, the National Association of Social Workers, and the American Psychiatric Association. Since that time, social and behavioral science research has significantly advanced our knowledge about lesbians, gay men, and bisexual people. Nevertheless, dominant cultural perspectives on same-sex erotic relationships in the United States continue to reflect stereotypes, and stigmatization and oppression of gay men and lesbians persist.

The contributors to this book believe that a deeper understanding of individual attitudes toward lesbians and gay men can be achieved by critically analyzing existing social and political systems for their current ideological implications. Our goal was to examine current indicators of heterosexism and homonegative attitudes, at multiple levels of analysis and representation, in order to better understand the cultural obstacles and openings to attitudinal transformation. Individual identities and relational behaviors can be legitimized or delegitimized at various levels in the dominant culture because collective ideologies, institutional policies, individual attitudes, and knowledge-gathering endeavors are mutually reflective and reciprocally influential processes. For example, the removal of homosexuality as a mental illness category by the American Psychiatric Association in 1973 was as much a representation of significant change in social values as it was a scientific response to objective data. Ultimately, eliminating anti-gay/lesbian prejudice depends, at least in part, upon our ability to elucidate the institutionalized meanings and values that either support or deny the need for such change.

Clearly, cultural constructions of attitudes toward gay men and lesbians are multifaceted and complex. The pervasiveness and widespread social acceptance of heterosexism demands critical investigation, but its very ubiquity in American culture also precludes a comprehensive analysis of every possible representation due to an exhaustless range of contexts. Thus, in this volume, each chapter author focuses on a particular manifestation of attitudes toward lesbians and gay men, and evaluates it from psychological, sociocultural, and/or institutional levels of analysis. The combined result represents complementary and interdisciplinary perspectives which blend empirical research, critical social analysis, individual and institutional case studies, and psychological theory.

Tracy Luchetta presents research findings regarding the relationship between negative attitudes toward gay men and lesbians and the tendency to stigmatize persons with HIV/AIDS. Francis Carleton analyzes various judicial perspectives regarding their contributions to the social construction of a collective identity for gay men and lesbians. Linda Gannon examines homophobia in academia through an analysis of institutional policy and practice, and through research on student attitudes. Elizabeth Johnson presents a framework for considering and addressing internalized homophobia in the context of therapeutic process and outcome. And finally, Lynn Pardie discusses the psychological foundations of heterosexism and the implications for spiritual development.

A consistent theme emerges in all chapters regarding the need for continuing efforts to identify heterosexism at sociocultural and individual levels, and for education in the service of promoting positive change. Although many academicians and researchers may be familiar with contemporary knowledge regarding sexual orientation, gender, and sexuality, it is clear that such information has not been widely integrated into mainstream American culture or individual identities. Attitudes are multiply determined, and resistance to change must be overcome on multiple levels for cultural transformation to occur. We hope that this book enhances understanding of the socially constructed meanings of heterosexism and homonegativity, and contributes to the development of greater respect for human diversity and differing social identities.

Sincere thanks are extended to Linda, Francis, and Liz for their fine contributions and to The Haworth Press, Inc., for their interest in publishing our work and their commitment to gay and lesbian studies. Lynn Pardie would also like to thank the University of Illinois at Springfield for providing support for this project.

Lynn Pardie
Tracy Luchetta

Chapter 1

Relationships Between Homophobia, HIV/AIDS Stigma, and HIV/AIDS Knowledge

Tracy Luchetta

Persons with HIV/AIDS have been and continue to be the targets of stigma due to their illness status as well as the association of the disease with already stigmatized groups (Herek and Glunt, 1988). Indeed, a significant minority of respondents in a representative random sample of adults in the United States expressed negative feelings toward persons with AIDS (PWAs). For example, between one-fourth and one-third of respondents admitted feelings of anger, disgust, and fear, and nearly half of all respondents stated that they would avoid the owner of a neighborhood grocery store if he or she had AIDS (Herek and Capitanio, 1993). Stigmatization of persons with HIV/AIDS cannot be explained adequately by the same processes underlying negative reactions to other stigmatized illnesses. In a meta-analysis of empirical studies that included measures of AIDS-related stigma compared to stigma associated with comparably serious illnesses, Crawford (1996) found a greater degree of stigma associated with AIDS when compared to cancer, hepatitis, herpes, heart disease, and drug abuse.

In this chapter, I briefly discuss the constructs of stigma and homophobia and identify possible theoretical links between AIDS-related stigma and negative attitudes toward lesbians and gay men using Herek's neo-functional approach to explanations of sexual

The author would like to thank Jennifer Marcks and Michael Satteson for their valuable assistance.

prejudice. Next, I summarize the current empirical literature concerning the relationships between attitudes toward lesbians and gay men, the tendency to stigmatize persons with AIDS, and current medical knowledge of AIDS. Finally, I present findings from a study of college students' attitudes toward lesbians, gays, and PWAs and their general knowledge about HIV/AIDS.

THE CONCEPT AND FUNCTIONS OF STIGMA

The definition of stigma as a mark or brand of shame has been elaborated by social scientists to refer to the social label conferred upon individuals or groups by virtue of their possession of a characteristic indicative of a deviant condition (Goffman, 1963). Goffman's and others' subsequent conceptualizations of stigma focus on the social contexts in which characteristics or attributes are transformed into grounds for social discredit and disqualification, and on the processes by which individuals become stigmatized (Jones et al., 1984). Therefore, stigmatization is essentially a relational construct; a stigmatized person must be marked or labeled as deviating from a social standard or norm, and the label must be socially constructed as negatively valued. An attributional component is inherent in most formulations of the stigma construct; the mark is regarded as the result or manifestation of a personal attribute, disposition, or trait. In other words, the stigmatized individual is perceived as guilty in some way for having caused or maintained their "marked" condition, even when no evidence for their culpability is readily apparent. When evidence of personal responsibility is lacking, observers tend to rely on stereotypical beliefs to make such attributions.

In the case of illness-related stigma, this conceptualization explains the greater degree of stigma attached to PWAs when compared to those with other infectious life-threatening illnesses, such as hepatitis (Crawford, 1996), as well as the relatively smaller degree of stigma accorded to PWAs who have contracted HIV through medical means of transmission, such as blood transfusion, rather than through sexual contact or intravenous (IV) drug use (D'Angelo et al., 1998; Leone and Wingate, 1991). In both comparisons, the group accorded greater stigma is held personally responsible for its condition because it has engaged in behaviors labeled deviant by the culture, such as same-sex sexual contact and illegal drug use.

Stereotyping is related to the stigma process in many important ways. Stereotypes are generally defined as overgeneralized, widely held, and typically negative beliefs about a social category or group. Stereotypes contribute to the stigmatization process in at least two ways. The first, as previously mentioned, occurs when stereotypical beliefs about a marked social category or group are used to justify attributing personal responsibility for the origin or maintenance of the stigmatized condition, even though causal evidence is lacking or ambiguous. For example, obese persons may be perceived as responsible for bringing on or maintaining their condition through voracity, in the absence of evidence of an uncontrollable cause, such as a medical condition or disorder. This stereotype—the belief that obese persons are insatiable overeaters—is an example of the phenomenon referred to as the fundamental attribution error, which is the tendency to view others' behavior as resulting from internal traits or characteristics rather than from external circumstances. This is a particularly Western cultural tendency (Miller, 1984; Morris and Peng, 1994) and serves to protect those who make such errors in judgment from perceiving themselves as vulnerable to the plight of less fortunate others or to the affliction of those who carry a potentially stigma-inducing mark.

A second and critical function of stereotypes in the stigmatization process is to explain or rationalize the negative affect that accompanies the devaluation of the stigmatized person (Jones et al., 1984). A theoretical framework for understanding the relationship between negative affect and the devaluation component of stigma can be found in the contemporary literature on attitudes. Attitudes are generally defined as overall evaluations of objects based on cognitive (e.g., stereotypical beliefs), affective (e.g., negative feelings about the object), and behavioral (e.g., tendencies toward avoidance or aggression) information. Negative beliefs about members of stigmatized groups serve to justify the affective component of attitudes toward them. According to Jones et al. (1984), "[negative] affect predisposes the individual to perceive and emphasize negative characteristics and attributions to explain one's discomfort or hostility" (p. 10).

To introduce a discussion of the purposes and functions of social stigma, I refer to a definition of stigma offered by Alonzo and Reynolds (1995) that synthesizes much of the contemporary discussion of the impact of stigma on stigmatized persons:

> . . . the stigmatized are a category of people who are pejoratively regarded by the broader society and who are devalued, shunned or otherwise lessened in their life chances and in access to the humanizing benefit of free and unfettered social intercourse. (p. 304)

The stigma process marks the boundaries between members of in-groups and deviants, who are then devalued and dehumanized, thus justifying prejudice and promoting in-group solidarity. Therefore, social stigmatization is one mechanism by which systems of sociocultural oppression are enacted and rationalized in social discourse.

THE CONCEPT AND FUNCTIONS OF NEGATIVE ATTITUDES TOWARD LESBIANS AND GAY MEN

The term *homophobia* was first introduced in 1967 to describe irrationally negative attitudes toward homosexual persons (Weinberg, 1972). Since that time, much evolution has occurred in the conceptualization and measurement of the construct. Various definitions can be found in the literature, which results in some controversy and confusion in terminology. One usage, which is narrowly based on the etymological structure of the word, defines homophobia as an "unreasoning fear of or antipathy toward homosexuals and homosexuality" (*Random House Webster's College Dictionary*, 1995, p. 642) and as the "dread of being in close proximity with a homosexual" (e.g., Bouton et al., 1987; Hudson and Ricketts, 1980; MacDonald, 1976). However, Herek (1986) and Kite (1994) argue that a fear-based definition of homophobia is problematic.

One problem in placing negative reactions toward homosexuals within the definitional scope of a phobic aversion is that homophobic persons do not always attempt to avoid being near a homosexual. This is apparent in instances of violence and hostility toward homosexuals. (After all, acrophobics don't attempt to destroy tall buildings or enact anti-skyscraper legislation.) While fear may be a component in negative attitudes toward homosexuals, a fear-based definition neglects other attitudinal components. Second, such a narrow definition fails to recognize the connections between negative attitudes toward homosexuals and other negative attitudes, perceptions, and prejudices. For example, homophobia has consistently been demonstrated to be related to a variety of attitudes and beliefs, including gender role attitudes, religious fundamentalism, and authoritarianism (Herek, 1994, 1995).

Other theorists favor broader conceptualizations of the term, and the extended parameters of the construct range from an attitude of condemnation against or prejudice toward gay men and lesbians to any negative attitude toward homosexuality. Alternative terminology includes *homonegativity* (Hudson and Ricketts, 1980) and *heterosexism* (Herek, 1986, 1995) to better represent the cultural context and attitudinal antecedents encompassed in theory and research about reactions to lesbians and gays. This expansion of the definition is favored by some and criticized by others. Kite (1994) argues that a more comprehensive definition allows for the " . . . consideration of reactions to lesbians and gay men as part of a broader framework of stereotyping and prejudice" (p. 28). Others point out that such all-encompassing definitions obscure the multidimensionality of the construct (O'Donohue and Caselles, 1993; Schwanberg, 1993). I argue for the position favoring a comprehensive conceptualization on the grounds that a complete understanding of the concept must take into consideration the cultural ideology that supports and is reflected by individual attitudes (Herek, 1995; Pharr, 1988). Consistent with this view is Herek's preference for the terms "heterosexisms" or "homophobias." This terminology recognizes the multidimensional nature of the construct and encompasses psychological heterosexism or homophobia, which emphasizes individual attitudes, and cultural heterosexism, which is reflected in institutional practices and norms that privilege heterosexuality over other forms of sexual expression and lifestyles (Herek, 1998).

Herek (1995) takes a functional approach to understanding individual differences in levels of psychological heterosexism and identifies various benefits of or needs served by holding negative attitudes toward gays and lesbians. The first function is an *experiential* one in the sense that attitudes are formed as a way of deriving meaning from experiences. Presumably, greater contact with openly gay men and lesbians would result in more favorable attitudes because such contact would allow persons to form attitudes based on actual experience rather than stereotypes. This prediction has been empirically supported by studies showing that interpersonal contact with lesbians and gay men is consistently related to more positive attitudes (Herek, 1994). However, this particular function would seem insufficient to explain most people's attitudes toward gays and lesbians because sexual orientation is not typically a conspicuous marker in mundane social interactions, nor are gay men or lesbians likely to indiscriminately disclose their identity status to individuals who may hold unfavorable attitudes toward them. Furthermore, the assumption that experience unidirectionally influences attitude formation is problematic without experimental (versus anecdotal) evidence. In studies relying solely upon self-report data, recollection of the valence of encounters with a particular group is likely to be contaminated by pre-existing stereotypes and prejudice. Finally, persons with pre-existing negative attitudes toward a particular group may proactively avoid contact with members of that group.

A second function of psychological heterosexism, according to Herek, involves strengthening one's *social identity* through either the expression of important personal values or the expression of values and beliefs of a group from whom one desires approval and acceptance. Ultimately, the social identity function of attitudes serves to increase feelings of self-esteem.

The third function of heterosexist attitudes is *ego-defensive*, referring to the reduction of anxiety one achieves by unconsciously projecting his or her internal conflicts (in this case, conflicts concerning sexuality and gender) onto an external target. This function appears to be the individual counterpart to one of the principle functions of the ideology of cultural heterosexism: " . . . the promotion by society in general of heterosexuality as the sole, legitimate expression of sexuality and affection" (Bohan, 1996, p. 39). Expressing negative attitudes toward gay men and lesbians is an assertion of one's own heterosexuality and adherence to norms for gender-related behaviors, and appears to underlie, at least in part, antigay violence (Franklin, 1998).

The earlier discussion of the role of stereotypes in attitude formation, combined with Herek's functional approach to heterosexist attitudes, provides a theoretical framework for elaborating upon the conceptual intersection between attitudes toward gay men and lesbians and attitudes toward PWAs. Given that homosexual behavior continues to be the predominant mode of HIV transmission in the United States (Centers for Disease Control and Prevention [CDC], 1997), HIV/AIDS is considered by many to be a disease exclusively affecting gay persons (see Herek, 1990, for a discussion of the sociohistorical context in which AIDS has been constructed as a disease affecting certain at-risk groups). Therefore, stereotypes about gays and lesbians are prone to be applied to PWAs and, when knowledge about HIV/AIDS is lacking or ambiguous, stereotypical beliefs may be used to justify attributing personal responsibility for the origin or maintenance of the illness and/or to rationalize negative affect aroused by the phenomenon. This process constitutes one pathway or mechanism by which stigma toward PWAs might have its origins in attitudes toward gay men and lesbians. Such a process provides a theoretical explanation for the observation that PWAs are more stigmatized than persons suffering from other, comparably serious, illnesses (Crawford, 1996), and the findings of recent studies indicating that AIDS stigma is less toward PWAs who are described as hemophiliac or heterosexual than those described as gay or IV drug abusers (D'Angelo et al., 1998; Johnson and Baer, 1996). This formulation is also supported by empirical data suggesting that the relationship between homophobic attitudes and AIDS-related attitudes is mediated by attributions of personal or moral blame for contracting the virus (Herek and Glunt, 1991).

The *experiential* function served by heterosexist attitudes can also explain, to some extent, the relationship between homonegativity and AIDS stigma. Lack of experience with, or knowledge about, PWAs would increase the likelihood of resorting to stereotypes when forming attitudes about PWAs. The characterization of HIV/AIDS as a disease predominantly affecting homosexuals would result in the overlapping of cognitive categories and the invocation of stereotypes about gays and lesbians in the formation of attitudes toward PWAs. This would be especially likely when knowledge is lacking or ambiguous. As indicated above, negative stereotyping is more likely to be exhibited by those who have little contact with members of stigmatized groups. This formulation is consistent with the finding that having friends or acquaintances who are gay, lesbian, or bisexual tends to be negatively related to fear of AIDS (Bouton et al., 1989; Miller, Briggs, and Corcoran, 1997). It also suggests a paired association between the category of PWAs and the category of gays, lesbians, and bisexuals and supports the experiential function underlying the expression of attitudes toward both categories.

The second function of homophobic attitudes, as discussed by Herek, involves the self-esteem enhancing *social identity* function. To the extent that persons subscribe to the *just world hypothesis* (the assumption that people generally get what they deserve) and also believe that homosexuality is immoral, PWAs may be viewed as getting what they deserve for engaging in morally reprehensible behaviors. This attribution may serve the social identity function by reinforcing one's belief system. At the same time, it may represent an attempt to bolster low self-esteem; by condemning homosexual behaviors and affirming one's heterosexual orientation, one is reassured of in-group status and moral superiority. This is consistent with the empirical finding that a negative attitude toward homosexual AIDS victims was related to a stronger belief in the just world hypothesis and poorer self-esteem (Glennon and Joseph, 1993).

The *ego-defensive* function of homophobic attitudes can also explain AIDS-related stigma in the sense that the paired association of AIDS with homosexual behavior might intensify negative stereotypes that portray gay persons and lesbians as dangerously abnormal, perverted (for example, gay men are stereotyped as sexually promiscuous; therefore, a gay man with HIV/AIDS is especially dangerous), or mentally ill (Kite, 1994). Such an association also links death anxiety to conflicts around sexual orientation and gender issues (Herek, 1990). Empirical support for the ego-defensive function of AIDS-related stigma was reported by Brandyberry and MacNair (1996), who found that college students' fear of AIDS was significantly predicted by fear of death and a defensive attitude toward AIDS. This function is also supported by studies showing that attitudes toward heterosexual PWAs tend to be more positive than toward homosexual PWAs (D'Angelo et al., 1998; Johnson and Baer, 1996), which can be interpreted to suggest that heterosexual persons judge heterosexual PWAs more favorably as a means of denying their own vulnerability to infection and the ensuing AIDS stigma.

PREVIOUS RESEARCH CONCERNING HOMOPHOBIA AND HIV/AIDS-RELATED ATTITUDES

An expanding body of research has demonstrated a relationship between attitudes toward lesbians and gay men and the tendency to stigmatize persons with HIV/AIDS (e.g., D'Augelli and Hershberger, 1995; Herek and Glunt, 1991; McDevitt et al., 1990; Young et al., 1991). College students' levels of homophobia also tend to be associated with knowledge concerning the medical aspects of AIDS (Bouton et al., 1989; Cline and Johnson, 1992; Johnson and Baer, 1996; Magruder, Whitbeck, and Ishii-Kuntz, 1993; Walters, 1997), because increased levels of homophobia are related to inaccuracies in knowledge about HIV/AIDS. One explanation for this relationship suggests that pre-existing homophobic attitudes lead people to select certain sources of information about AIDS that might be inaccurate or that reinforce stereotypes they hold about PWAs, and screen out others that might be reliable. Another explanation hypothesizes that public information sources about AIDS have associated the disease with homosexual behavior, contributing to the belief that homosexuals are responsible for the epidemic (Magruder et al., 1993). Magruder and colleagues investigated the contribution of various sources of information about HIV/AIDS to general homophobic attitudes and accuracy of knowledge about AIDS. They found that information from churches and discussions with friends were associated with decreased accuracy of knowledge about AIDS and with increased levels of homophobia.

THE PRESENT STUDY

The goals of the present study were twofold. First, I sought to replicate previous findings showing a relationship between attitudes toward lesbians and gay men and toward PWAs. I expected college students' homophobic attitudes to be associated with the tendency to stigmatize PWAs. Because research data concerning HIV and AIDS information are continually changing and expanding, there is a need for replicating and updating studies assessing AIDS knowledge. Since the perception of AIDS as an exclusively "gay disease" is becoming increasingly less accurate, my second goal was to investigate the relationship between college students' general knowledge about the medical aspects of AIDS and homophobia. Thus, I hypothesized that the accuracy of students' general factual information about AIDS would vary according to their levels of homophobia.

Method

Participants

I administered a collection of self-report instruments to undergraduate students enrolled in human development courses at a mid-sized comprehensive university in the midwestern United States. A total of 178 students participated; however, only those who indicated a heterosexual orientation were included, resulting in a sample of 166 participants. Of this sample, 85.5 percent ($n = 142$) were women, and 97 percent were white. The average age of the participants was 22.8 years (range 18 to 46). In terms of religious affiliation, 54 percent were Roman Catholic, 20 percent were Protestant, and the remaining respondents endorsed *other, none,* or *Jewish.* Seventy-eight percent of this sample reported that they were single, and 20 percent were married or cohabitating.

Instruments

Attitudes toward lesbians and gay men scale-short form (ATLG-S). This scale contains ten items and comprises two subscales (ATL-S and ATG-S) which assess homophobia as attitudes of condemnation against or prejudice toward gay men and lesbians (Herek, 1984, 1994). Herek (1994) summarized the development of this scale and described numerous studies evaluating its reliability and validity, as well as establishing the instrument as a criterion for assessing heterosexuals' attitudes toward lesbians and gay men. Previous studies using the ATLG-S have reported alpha coefficients of .87 to .91 for the ATG-S, .85 to .87 for the ATL-S, and .92 for the ATLG-S

(Herek, 1994). Correlations between each subscale and its full-length counterpart have been reported as .95, .96, and .97 for the ATL-S, the ATG-S, and the ATLG-S, respectively, attesting to the equivalency of each short-form subscale with the longer version (Herek, 1994). The instrument has been used with student as well as community samples, and scores have consistently been shown to correlate with a variety of attitudinal variables, including gender role beliefs and religious fundamentalism (Herek, 1994).

For the present study, respondents were instructed to rate their agreement/disagreement with each item along a five-point rating scale (1 = *strongly disagree;* 5 = *strongly agree*). Two separate scores were computed for items targeting gay men (ATG-S) and lesbians (ATL-S). Higher scores indicate greater levels of homo-negativity. The mean subscale scores for this sample were 11.75 (range 5 to 22; *SD* = 4.19) for the ATL-S and 12.68 (range 5 to 25; *SD* = 5.32) for the ATG-S. Alpha coefficients were .84 and .91 for the ATL-S and ATG-S, respectively.

Attitudes about lesbians and female homosexuality/attitudes about gay men and male homosexuality. Designed to measure individuals' attitudes toward homosexuals and homosexuality, these scales were specifically developed to address conceptual and methodological flaws in the construction of previous scales (Daly, 1989). Close attention was paid to rigorous procedures for item selection and analysis, establishing reliability and validity, and cross-validation. The inventory consists of two subscales, each consisting of sixteen statements to which the respondent is asked to indicate agreement on a 5-point Likert-type scale (1 = *strongly disagree;* 5 = *strongly agree*). Higher scores indicate more negative attitudes toward lesbians and/or gay men. The author of the instrument reported alpha coefficients of .94 for the Attitudes About Lesbians and Female Homosexuality (L) subscale and .95 for the Attitudes About Gay Men and Male Homosexuality (G) subscale. Factor analysis revealed unidimensional structures for each scale. In the present sample, alpha coefficients were .93 for scale L and .92 for scale G.

Attitudes about AIDS scale (AAAS). The AAAS is a twenty-four-item scale assessing the tendency for persons to stigmatize PWAs (Trezza, 1994). For example, one item states, "AIDS patients offend me morally." Higher scores indicate greater levels of stigma.

General AIDS information questionnaire (GAIQ). The original GAIQ consisted of forty-eight statements concerning the medical aspects of AIDS. For each statement, the respondent was asked to indicate *true, false,* or *don't know* (Trezza, 1994). I modified the GAIQ from the author's original version to reflect recent medical and epidemiological findings about the HIV/AIDS virus and epidemic. For example, I added the statements, "Heterosexual transmission of HIV via vaginal intercourse occurs more often from female to male than from male to female" (false), and "In the United States, AIDS is increasing more rapidly among women than among men" (true). Correct responses were summed (*don't know* was considered incorrect), so that higher scores indicated more accurate knowledge.

Results

Comparisons of mean scores by gender for all homophobia scales revealed no significant differences between men and women on any of the homophobia subscales (see Table 1.1). Within-gender comparisons have previously demonstrated a tendency for men to score higher on subscales targeting gay men as compared to their attitudes toward lesbians, while the reverse tends to be true for women (Kite,

TABLE 1.1. Mean Scores by Gender on Scales Assessing Attitudes Toward Lesbians and Gay Men

Scale	Means (SD)		t-tests for independent samples
	Women (n = 142)	Men (n = 24)	
ATG–S	12.4 (5.3)[a]	14.2 (5.6)[c]	-1.46 *ns*
ATL–S	11.8 (4.2)[a]	11.2 (4.2)[c]	.74 *ns*
G	36.3 (11.4)[b]	39.5 (12.8)	-1.23 *ns*
L	42.2 (13.5)[b]	40.9 (11.5)	.43 *ns*

Notes: ATG-S = Attitudes Toward Gay Men Scale–Short Form; ATL-S = Attitude Toward Lesbians Scale-Short Form; G = Attitudes About Gay Men and Male Homosexuality; L = Attitudes About Lesbians and Female Homosexuality. Means having the same superscript differ significantly at $p < .001$ by paired sample t-tests.

1984). In this sample, the women scored nearly one standard deviation higher on Daly's Attitudes About Lesbians and Female Homosexuality subscale than on the corresponding subscale targeting gay men. Contrary to expectations, mean differences between Herek's ATG-S and ATL-S subscales showed that women scored significantly (but marginally) higher on ATG-S than on ATL-S. For men, the mean score for Herek's ATG-S scale was significantly higher than the mean for the ATL-S scale. Intercorrelations among homophobia scales ranged from .85 to .89, which suggests high concordance among these scales. Students' general knowledge about the medical aspects of AIDS was reasonably accurate (GAIQ M = 35.8, or 75 percent correct). However, some specific knowledge deficits were observed; for example, only forty-three percent of respondents were aware that, in the United States, AIDS is increasing more rapidly among women than among men.

Correlations between homophobia scales, the AAAS, and the GAIS indicated tht higher levels of homophobia significantly predicted a tendency to stigmatize PWAs, and less accuracy in general knowledge about AIDS (see Table 1.2). Other descriptive variables were examined to determine the relationship between demographic characteristics and variables of interest in this study. First, the sample was divided into two groups: one group comprised those individuals reporting no knowledge of friends or family members who

TABLE 1.2. Intercorrelations Between Measures of Attitudes Toward Lesbians and Gay Men, the Attitudes About AIDS Scale, and the General AIDS Information Questionnaire

Scales	AAAS	GAIQ
ATG-S	.63***	-.24**
ATL-S	.60***	-.25**
G	.67***	-.21**
L	.63***	-.25**

Notes: ATG-S = Attitudes Toward Gay Men Scale-Short Form; ATL-S = Attitudes Toward Lesbians Scale-Short Form; G = Attitudes About Gay Men and Male Homosexuality; L = Attitudes About Lesbians and Female Homosexuality. N ranged from 150 to 163. **p < .01; ***p < .001.

are gay men or lesbians ($n = 66$); the other group consisted of those respondents reporting having at least one gay male or lesbian friend or family member ($n = 100$). Predictably, participants with at least one gay male or lesbian friend or family member scored significantly ($p < .05$) lower than the other group on three of the four homophobia scales (Daly's G and L scales and Herek's ATLS scale). Having a gay male or lesbian friend or family member did not matter regarding the tendency to stigmatize PWAs nor in terms of knowledge of the medical aspects of HIV/AIDS. Personal contact with PWAs (defined as *anyone with AIDS or who is HIV-positive*; scored as a dichotomous variable with values of *yes* or *no*) was not related to any of the homophobia scales, to the tendency to stigmatize PWAs, nor to knowledge of the medical aspects of AIDS.

Discussion

Negative attitudes toward lesbians and gay men existed long before HIV disease and AIDS became commonplace in the public discourse. The results of this study show that pre-existing homophobic or heterosexist attitudes may influence the way in which persons with HIV and AIDS may be unjustly treated, potentially increasing the burden of the disease itself. Negative attitudes may also interfere with accurate information processing and retention, as well as with assessments of potential risk or vulnerability to HIV and AIDS infection. Educators and health care professionals are advised to consider the importance of homophobic attitudes as a possible barrier to effective educational programs designed to prevent HIV and AIDS through the dissemination of accurate information.

One of the most striking conclusions to be drawn from the literature review and present findings is that homophobic or heterosexist attitudes are extensively embedded in our cultural norms and belief systems. As Bohan (1996) succinctly notes, a considerable body of literature has documented that homonegativity is associated with a number of individual characteristics and attitudinal variables, as well as with attitudes toward PWAs. Psychologists have applied theoretical models of the structure and functions of attitudes to understand the intrapersonal and interpersonal dynamics of homophobias and heterosexisms, as well as other related attitudes and prejudices. While such attempts are to be commended for their value in expanding knowledge and suggesting means of altering attitudes at the individual level, much work needs to be done to raise awareness of the reciprocal and interdependent relationships between psychological and cultural heterosexisms. Consider the passage of the Defense of Marriage Act by the 1996 U.S. Congress, which prohibits federal benefits for spouses in same-sex marriages, as well as reports of anti-gay/lesbian violence (Herek, 1995; Herek and Berrill, 1992; Kite, 1994). And, more recently, the House of Representatives approved measures that would deny federal housing funds to San Francisco because of its support of partner benefits to homosexual employees, and would take funding away from housing programs for people with AIDS (Berke, 1998).

The stigmatization of gay men, lesbians, persons with HIV/AIDS, and other "social deviants" can be understood on both individual and cultural levels: attitudes are the psychological expression and manifestation of multiple and interlocking cultural oppressions. The common elements of the various forms of oppression have been articulated elsewhere (Pharr, 1988), but the cultural embeddedness of the stigmatization of PWAs is well-illustrated by the fact that the list of groups disproportionately affected by HIV/AIDS is expanding to include ethnic minorities such as African-Americans, particularly African-American women (CDC, 1998). This epitomizes the way in which social and economic factors such as poverty, underemployment, and poor access to health care compound the stigma status of an already stigmatized group.

Although the stigmatization process is but one manifestation of oppression, it is an important mechanism by which individual and cultural oppressions exert reciprocal influence. The cause of cultural transformation in the direction of social justice is served if scholars, educators, activists, political leaders, and citizens recognize the common elements of oppression and work toward eliminating both individual and cultural manifestations of stigma toward all oppressed groups.

REFERENCES

Alonzo, A. A. and Reynolds, N. R. (1995). Stigma, HIV and AIDS: An exploration and elaboration of a stigma trajectory. *Social Science and Medicine, 41*(3), 303-315.

Berke, R. L. (1998). Chasing the polls on gay rights. *The New York Times,* August 2, sec. 4, p. 3.

Bohan, J. S. (1996). *Psychology and sexual orientation: Coming to terms.* New York: Routledge.

Bouton, R. A., Gallaher, P. E., Garlinghouse, P. A., Leal, T., Rosenstein, L. D., and Young, R. K. (1987). Scales for measuring fear of AIDS and homophobia. *Journal of Personality Assessment, 51*(4), 606-614.

Bouton, R. A., Gallaher, P. E., Garlinghouse, P. A., Leal, T., Rosenstein, L. D., and Young, R. K. (1989). Demographic variables associated with fear of AIDS and homophobia. *Journal of Applied Social Psychology, 19*(11), 885-901.

Brandyberry, L. J. and MacNair, R. R. (1996). The content and function of attitudes toward AIDS. *Journal of College Student Development, 37*(3), 335-346.

Centers for Disease Control and Prevention (1997). *HIV/AIDS surveillance report, 9*(2).

Centers for Disease Control and Prevention (1998). *Update: For African-Americans, (Americans,* June).

Cline, R. J. W., and Johnson, S. J. (1992). Mosquitoes, doorknobs, and sneezing: Relationships between homophobia and AIDS mythology among college students. *Health Communication, 4*(4), 273-289.

Crawford, A. M. (1996). Stigma associated with AIDS: A meta-analysis. *Journal of Applied Social Psychology, 26*(5), 398-416.

Daly, J. (1989). *Measuring attitudes toward lesbians and gay men: Development and initial psychometric evaluation of an instrument.* Unpublished doctoral dissertation, Southern Illinois University, Carbondale.

D'Angelo, R. J., McGuire, J. M., Abbott, D. W., and Sheridan, K. (1998). Homophobia and perceptions of people with AIDS. *Journal of Applied Social Psychology, 28*(2), 157-170.

D'Augelli, A. R., and Hershberger, S. L. (1995). A multiyear analysis of changes in AIDS concerns and homophobia on a university campus. *Journal of College Health, 44*(1), 3-10.

Franklin, K. (1998). Unassuming motivations: Contextualizing the narratives of anti-gay assailants. In G. M. Herek (Ed.), *Psychological perspectives on lesbian and gay issues: Volume 4. Stigma and sexual orientation: Understanding prejudice against lesbians, gay men, and bisexuals* (pp. 1-23). Thousand Oaks, CA: Sage.

Glennon, F. and Joseph, S. (1993). Just world beliefs, self-esteem, and attitudes towards homosexuals with AIDS. *Psychological Reports, 72*(2), 584-586.

Goffman, E. (1963). *Stigma: Notes on the management of spoiled identity.* Englewood Cliffs, NJ: Prentice-Hall.

Herek, G. M. (1984). Beyond homophobia: A social psychological perspective on attitudes towards lesbians and gay men. *Journal of Homosexuality, 10*(1/2), 1-21.

Herek, G. M. (1986). The social psychology of homophobia: Toward a practical theory. *Review of Law and Social Change, 14*(4), 923-934.

Herek, G. M. (1990). Illness, stigma, and AIDS. In P. T. Costa, Jr., and G. R. VandenBos (Eds.), *Psychological aspects of serious illness: Chronic condi-*

tions, fatal diseases, and clinical care (pp. 103-150). Washington, DC: American Psychological Association.

Herek, G. M. (1994). Assessing heterosexuals' attitudes toward lesbian and gay men: A review of empirical research with the ATLG scale. In B. Greene and G. M. Herek (Eds.), *Psychological perspectives on lesbian and gay issues: Volume 1. Lesbian and gay psychology: Theory, research, and clinical applications* (pp. 206-228). Thousand Oaks, CA: Sage.

Herek, G. M. (1995). Psychological heterosexism in the United States. In A. R. D'Augelli and C. J. Patterson (Eds.), *Lesbian, gay, and bisexual identities over the lifespan: Psychological perspectives* (pp. 321-346). New York: Oxford.

Herek, G. M. (1998, August). *Sexual prejudice: The social psychology of homophobias and heterosexisms.* Paper presented at the meeting of the American Psychological Association, San Francisco, CA.

Herek, G. M. and Berrill, K. T. (Eds.). (1992). *Hate crimes: Confronting violence against lesbians and gay men.* Newbury Park, CA: Sage.

Herek, G. M. and Capitanio, J. P. (1993). Public reactions to AIDS in the United States: A second decade of stigma. *American Journal of Public Health, 83*(4), 574-577.

Herek, G. M. and Glunt, E. K. (1988). An epidemic of stigma. *American Psychologist, 43*(11), 886-891.

Herek, G. M. and Glunt, E. K. (1991). AIDS-related attitudes in the Unites States: A preliminary conceptualization. *The Journal of Sex Research, 28*(1), 99-123.

Hudson, W. and Ricketts, W. (1980). A strategy for the measurement of homophobia. *Journal of Homosexuality, 5*(4), 357-372.

Johnson, M. E. and Baer, A. J. (1996). College students' judgments and perceptions of persons with AIDS from different risk groups. *The Journal of Psychology, 130*(5), 527-536.

Jones, E. E., Farina, A., Hastorf, A. H., Markus, H., Miller, D. T., and Scott, R. A. (1984). *Social stigma: The psychology of marked relationships.* New York: W. H. Freeman.

Kite, M. E. (1984). Sex differences in attitudes toward homosexuals: A meta-analytic review. *Journal of Homosexuality, 10*(1/2), 69-81.

Kite, M. E. (1994). When perceptions meet reality: Individual differences in reactions to lesbians and gay men. In B. Greene and G. M. Herek (Eds.), *Psychological perspectives on lesbian and gay issues: Volume 1. Lesbian and gay psychology: Theory, research, and clinical applications* (pp. 25-53). Thousand Oaks, CA: Sage.

Leone, C. and Wingate, C. (1991). A functional approach to understanding attitudes toward AIDS victims. *The Journal of Social Psychology, 131*(6), 761-768.

MacDonald, A. P. (1976). Homophobia: Its roots and meanings. *Homosexual Counseling Journal, 3*(1), 23-33.

Magruder, B., Whitbeck, L. B., and Ishii-Kuntz, M. (1993). The relationship between AIDS-related information sources and homophobic attitudes: A comparison of two models. *Journal of Homosexuality, 25*(4), 47-68.

McDevitt, T. M., Sheehan, E. P., Lennon, R., and Ambrosio, A. L. (1990). Correlates of attitudes toward AIDS. *Journal of Social Psychology, 130*(5), 699-701.

Miller, D. B., Briggs, H. and Corcoran, K. (1997). Fear of AIDS and homophobia scales: Additional estimates of reliability and validity. *Psychological Reports, 81*(3), 783-786.

Miller, J. G. (1984). Culture and the development of everyday social explanation. *Journal of Personality and Social Psychology, 46*(5), 961-978.

Morris, M. W. and Peng, K. (1994). Culture and cause: American and Chinese attributions for social and physical events. *Journal of Personality and Social Psychology, 67*(6), 949-971.

O'Donohue, W. and Caselles, C. E. (1993). Homophobia: Conceptual, definitional, and value issues. *Journal of Psychopathology and Behavioral Assessment, 15*(3), 177-195.

Pharr, S. (1988). *Homophobia: A weapon of sexism.* Little Rock, AR: The Women's Project.

Random House Webster's College Dictionary. (1995). New York: Random House.

Schwanberg, S. L. (1993). Attitudes toward gay men and lesbian women: Instrumentation issues. *Journal of Homosexuality, 26*(1), 99-136.

Trezza, G. R. (1994). HIV knowledge and stigmatization of persons with AIDS: Implications for the development of HIV education for young adults. *Professional Psychology: Research and Practice, 25*(2), 141-148.

Walters, A. S. (1997). The influence of homophobia in HIV/AIDS education. *Journal of Psychology and Human Sexuality, 9*(2), 17-38.

Weinberg, G. (1972). *Society and the healthy homosexual.* New York: St. Martin's.

Young, R. K., Gallaher, P., Belasco, J., Barr, A., and Webber, A. W. (1991). Changes in fear of AIDS and homophobia in a university population. *Journal of Applied Social Psychology, 21*(22), 1848-1858.

Chapter 2

Contested Identity:
The Law's Construction
of Gay and Lesbian Subjects

Francis Carleton

Alexis de Tocqueville observed, back in the early nineteenth century, that "scarcely any political question arises in the United States that is not resolved, sooner or later, into a judicial question" (Tocqueville, 1835/1948, p. 280). He went on to note that "the spirit of the law, which is produced in the schools and courts of justice, gradually penetrates . . . into the bosom of society" (p. 280). It is the premise of this chapter that the law is thus a critical battleground in the struggle over gay and lesbian rights. Although it is apparent that much of the judiciary's power lies in its ability to make public policy, perhaps the most important sense in which the law is a crucial factor in the success of any social movement is its ability to legitimize, or delegitimize, the way people think about the issues surrounding that movement. The law can either reinforce the beliefs that people have about a particular issue, or it can encourage them to change their beliefs.

One might argue that the most important impact of the landmark Supreme Court case of *Brown v. Board of Education* (1954) was its long-term undermining of the belief that segregated schools in the South were desirable and proper. The Supreme Court's attack upon the doctrine of *separate but equal* led, in the long run, to society's rejection of such a system. Foster believes that the struggle to secure gay and lesbian rights via the courts is itself symbolic. Efforts to effect broad social change in the judicial domain have served "to confer a greater degree of mainstream acceptance and integration . . . in a society that has too often viewed us as outsiders" (Foster, 1998, p. 321). Examples of these efforts include the struggle for the legitimization of same-sex marriages and protection under federal civil rights laws. In this chapter I will focus on law as ideology—as a key institution that both reflects and shapes how society defines particular groups of people. I believe that these cultural understandings ultimately play a key role in shaping broader struggles over the distribution of political and social power in local, state, and national communities. In short, I argue that ideas matter.

Cruikshank (1992) has argued that homophobia "cannot be eradicated by individual changes of heart but only by institutional change" (p. 93). However, we must also consider how institutional change can enhance the possibility of individual changes of heart because individual and institutional levels of change are not independent. That is, if the gay and lesbian civil rights movement can help move the law in the direction of recognizing the complex humanity of homosexuals, then individuals in society, gay and straight alike, will be more likely to subscribe to such a humanistic vision. It is all too apparent that society's condemnation of homosexuals has resulted in a significant degree of self-hatred on the part of gay and lesbian youth; they are roughly three times as likely as straight teenagers to attempt suicide, are more likely to suffer from drug and alcohol abuse, and so forth (D'Augelli, 1998). Both internalized and externalized homophobia take a terrible toll on the gay, lesbian, and bisexual communities.

Clearly one cannot reasonably expect the courts, in cases involving homosexuality, to capture the full complexity of the gay, lesbian, and bisexual identity of these subjects. Such a project is daunting for anyone—it is probably impossible to pin down the identity of any single individual, let alone an entire class of people. This is perhaps especially true in the wake of the postmodern critique of such a project. As Gagnier (1990) states, "in postmodernist theory, categories like race, class, or gender are too reductive to describe the complexity of social identities" (p. 23). As such, when I use the term *identity*, my expectations are relatively modest. I hope to analyze the extent to which the courts make a good-faith effort to paint a reasonably accurate and fact-dense portrait of those subjects who come before them—in the cases I examine below, of course, this means gay and lesbian individuals. And although there is merit to the postmodern attack upon identity construction using broad categories, I think that, realistically, we do at least attempt to make sense of each other through the invocation of such social and biological constructs as race and gender. Given this reality then, it becomes important, in the real world in which we all live, to pay attention to identity construction—even if, in an ideal sense, such a task is impossible.

A close examination of how courts identify gay and lesbian subjects will allow us to gauge, however roughly, the evolution, or lack thereof, of societal attitudes regarding these citizens. The legal ideology espoused by the courts does, in indirect but remarkably steady ways, reflect broader trends in society at large. Consider, for example, the Supreme Court's tragically unfortunate response to McCarthyism in the early 1950s; free speech rights went by the wayside in the court case of *Dennis v. United States* (1951), a case in which the Supreme Court upheld the federal conviction, under the Smith Act of 1940, of eleven leaders of the American Communist party for their teaching and advocacy of ideas that the government deemed dangerous, and in *Korematsu v. United States* (1944) the Court allowed the "relocation" of Japanese Americans to camps in the western deserts after the bombing of Pearl Harbor. For better or for worse, the courts do respond, however imperfectly, to the broad currents of public opinion. As such, the courts become another critical battleground in a high-stakes contest over what shape society will take. Indeed, one legal scholar has suggested that "legal discourse is itself a site for ongoing interpretive struggle over the meaning of identity" (Danielsen, 1995, p. 58). I will attempt to analyze this struggle in the following pages.

Cruikshank (1992) has pointed out that "victory for gay and lesbian liberation will come when most heterosexuals regard homosexuals as fully human, a change that will not automatically result from legal reform" (p. 195). Certainly this is true, but it is also true that the courts can play a significant role in either promoting or undermining a complex and positive social image of gay and lesbian people. As Nava and Dawidoff (1994) argue, "The majority culture's attachment to its stereotypes of gay men and women constitutes the single greatest impediment to gay and lesbian civil rights" (p. 29). As such, the law becomes an important battleground over the public's perception of the identity of gay and lesbian individuals. For example, if the law endorses and promotes the idea that gays are radically different from heterosexuals and devalues that difference, then the gay civil rights agenda can be defined successfully by opponents as an unwarranted intrusion on attempts by "straight" society to defend itself from threats posed by stigmatized groups. If, on the other hand, the courts can promote "if not admiration, at least some appreciation of the lives homosexuals live," then the gay and lesbian civil rights movement stands a far better chance of success (Sandel, 1989, p. 537).

Finally, if the courts, when dealing with gay and lesbian issues, choose to downplay and even ignore the fact that the subjects are gay, and do so by relying on technical statutory or constitutional interpretation, then several consequences seem possible. One possibility is that the gay subject will be erased and silenced, at least symbolically, by the law. Conversely, a legally neutral approach to sexual orientation may provide the collective gay and lesbian community the opportunity to define, in all of its infinite complexity and pluralism, an identity as multidimensional human beings. Another possibility is that such a neutral stance may open the door to social conservatives' continued demonization of the gay and lesbian community and to an erosion of that community's collective rights and liberties.

In this chapter, I will critically analyze several federal and state court cases dealing with gay and lesbian subjects. These cases are not meant to be comprehensive in scope, but instead are intended to illustrate how courts convey a variety of views regarding group identity for gay and lesbian subjects. The cases I analyze include the Wisconsin Supreme Court case of *Holtzman v. Knott* (1995), the U.S. Supreme Court cases of *Bowers v. Hardwick* (1986), and *Romer v. Evans* (1996), and the Ninth Circuit Court of Appeals case of *Watkins v. United States Army* (1988).

Various representations of gays and lesbians have been articulated by the courts in recent years. These can be summarized and interpreted according to three basic approaches used by the courts in cases dealing with gay and lesbian subjects. The first approach involves the use of *negative legal imagery*, wherein the courts draw a portrait of gay and lesbian people that is stereotypically dismissive of their actual identities. Others have referred to this as "scourge rhetoric" (Jacobs, 1993, p. 730). I will analyze carefully the majority opinion authored by Justice White and a concurring opinion by Chief Justice Burger in the infamous Supreme Court case of *Bowers v. Hardwick* (1986) to exemplify and explore this legal ideology. I will also draw from Scalia's dissent in *Romer v. Evans* (1996). Another approach sometimes utilized by courts is that of *positive endorsement*, whereby they attempt to describe accurately and humanely the lives of gay and lesbian people. Jacobs (1993) has referred to this as "affirmational rhetoric" (p. 729). For this category of legal ideology, I will discuss Justice Blackmun's dissenting opinion in *Bowers* and the majority opinion in a Ninth Circuit Court of Appeals case, *Watkins v. United States Army* (1988). Finally, there exists a class of cases in which courts deal with gay and lesbian issues but never really address explicitly the identity of the subjects in question. I refer to this approach as one of *legal neutrality*. For this model, I will draw from the majority opinion in the Supreme Court case of *Romer v. Evans* and an adoption case decided by the Wisconsin Supreme Court, *Holtzman v. Knott*.

AN ANALYSIS OF SEXUAL ORIENTATION JURISPRUDENCE

Negative Legal Imagery

In *Bowers v. Hardwick* (1986), the Supreme Court considered the constitutionality of a Georgia state law that criminalized sodomy, which is defined as contact between the sexual organ of one person and the mouth or anus of a partner. Mr. Hardwick was arrested while having sex with a male partner in the privacy of his own bedroom. He was apprehended by a police officer who had entered his house, with the consent of a roommate, and then pushed open an unlocked bedroom door on the pretext of delivering a court summons for violating an open container law some weeks earlier. The lower courts ruled that the Georgia anti-sodomy statute violated the privacy rights of Mr. Hardwick and so could not stand. The Supreme Court reversed this holding and, by a 5 to 4 vote, upheld the law in question as a legitimate intrusion on the privacy rights of gay citizens, which were apparently perceived to be of minimal importance.

Bowers has been described as a case that "looms over sexual orientation law like a brooding and malevolent omnipresence" (Coombs, 1996, p. 243). Mohr (1988) argues that *Bowers* "allowed the state to use law as invective against gays" (p. 315). Certainly this is the Court's best-known case involving gay and lesbian rights. In this case, the Court's majority opinion constructed a decidedly negative image of gay and lesbian citizens by directing stigmatic rhetoric at the object of its disaffection.

Justice White, author of the Court's majority opinion, emphasized the identity of gay and lesbian people. He made it clear from the start that the Court's recent history of upholding general privacy rights against government intrusion did not extend to gay citizens. Justice White referred to such landmark privacy cases as *Eisenstadt*,[1] *Roe*,[2] and *Griswold*,[3] and made it clear that the present case's subject did not fall under the protective umbrella constructed by the court. (The plaintiffs vindicated in the three aforementioned cases were all presumably heterosexual.) We can see in this differentiation, at least implicitly, the idea that heterosexual citizens have access to privacy rights when transacting very personal business, but homosexual individuals, because they are perceived to be thoroughly different, and different in a negative way, are given no such protection from the will of the majority.

Justice White also made explicit what he had, at first, only hinted at—that "no connection between family, marriage, or procreation. . . and homosexual activity. . . has been demonstrated" (*Bowers v. Hardwick*, 1986, p. 191). From this perspective, constitutional privacy rights are only legitimate when attached to family, marriage, or procreation; therefore, gay citizens enjoy no constitutional protection from statutes such as the one challenged in Georgia. Clearly, White constructed an aggressively negative image of gay people by summarily disenfranchising them from several of society's most important institutions and activities. By so doing, he dehumanized them and placed them beyond the pale of judicial protection. He also created a reductionistic definition of homosexual activity that presumably encompasses only the particular *sexual* activities that fall under Georgia's anti-sodomy law. In White's view, homosexuals are wholly defined by their intimate couplings with partners of the same sex, and homosexuals bear no relationship at all to family, marriage, or procreation. Hence, they are not a protected class under the provisions of the Constitution.

Justice White articulates in *Bowers* a relentlessly negative stereotype of gays which contrasts sharply with the actual identities of the subjects in question. One might respond to White's diatribe by pointing out that homosexual activity encompasses life-affirming and often mundane acts such as washing the dishes, walking the dog, shopping at the local produce market, attending family get-togethers, creating alternative families, committing to marriage-like relationships, and so forth. Along similar lines, Butler (1998) argues that White's narrow definition of family "fails to account for the significant number of gay and lesbian couples who do produce children, through insemination, surrogate parenthood, adoption, or previous marriages" (p. 868). Furthermore, it hardly seems fair to excoriate gay couples for not participating in marriage when many in the homosexual community have been fighting for access to this institution for many years. In short, it is clear that Justice White's attempt to define gay individuals as purely sexual beings who play no role in marriage, procreation, or family is demonstrably false. While Justice White may have been merely making official and explicit what many people in society believe quite reflexively, he exacerbated this situation by putting the Supreme Court's considerable prestige and power behind a profoundly negative and dehumanizing vision of gay and lesbian people. Surely this legalized homophobia can only place another barrier in the way of gay/lesbian/bisexual civil rights in the United States.

Another example of Justice White's denigration of gay and lesbian identity can be found in a passage in which he argued that the Court must be prepared to draw clear, bright lines regarding what is a legitimate and constitutionally protected right. White opined that if the Court extended judicial protection to gay sexual conduct, then "it would be difficult, except by fiat, to limit the claimed right to homosexual conduct while leaving exposed to prosecution adultery, incest, and other sexual crimes. . . . We are unwilling to start down that road" (*Bowers v. Hardwick*, 1986, pp. 195-196). White thus equated gay sex with incest and other sexual crimes beyond the pale of civilized conduct. Justice White thereby demonized the private lives of gay individuals and defined them as sexual criminals unworthy of protection from majoritarian regulations.

In a concurring opinion, Chief Justice Burger added to the massively negative and stereotypical imagery constructed by White. He reviewed the condemnation of homosexual practices in ancient Rome and in England under King Henry VIII, as well as the seminal English jurist Blackstone's discussion of homosexuality. In fact, Burger noted with approval Blackstone's argument that sodomy represents a more serious violation of the law than rape. We can probably safely assume that Burger meant this only in the context of homosexual, not heterosexual, sodomy. Burger concluded his highly selective review of Western history by noting that the Court must not "cast aside millennia of moral teaching" by striking down Georgia's anti-sodomy statute (*Bowers v. Hardwick*, 1986, p. 197). However, it should be noted that he does not similarly endorse the millennia of moral teaching, originating at least with Aristotle (1943), that slavery is right and just, although the parallel for devaluing human rights is clear. Burger also declined to consider Boswell's 1980 volume on gay history, which suggested that "the Roman Catholic Church had not condemned gay people throughout its history, but rather, at least until the twelfth century, had alternately evinced no special concern about homosexuality or actually celebrated love between men" (Chauncey, Duberman, and Vicinus, 1989, p. 5). Chief Justice Burger protested that he wished merely to endorse judicial deference to state legislative authority, but it is quite evident that he supported fully that element of Western history that relegated gays to the scrap heap.

Justice Scalia's dissent in *Romer v. Evans* also articulated a decidedly negative portrait of the gay and lesbian community; however, it must be noted that his anger, while clearly present, did not equal the sheer vitriol and hatred of the *Bowers* majority and concurring opinions. Neither White nor Burger made any serious attempt to construct a legal argument for the denial of gay and lesbian rights. Scalia's dissent in *Romer*, on the other hand, is attentive to legal arguments, while at the same time it undermines, albeit subtly, the collective identity of gay and lesbian citizens. Scalia's dissent (joined, not surprisingly, by Chief Justice Rehnquist and Justice Thomas) was written in response to the majority's decision, in *Romer,* to strike down Colorado's Amendment 2. Amendment 2 would have forbidden state and local laws protecting gays, lesbians, and bisexuals from discrimination. Justice Scalia sought to counter the majority's denigration of Amendment 2 supporters by arguing that Amendment 2 represented "a modest attempt by seemingly tolerant Coloradans to preserve traditional sexual mores against the efforts of a politically powerful minority to revise those mores through use of the laws" (*Romer v. Evans,* 1996, p. 636). At the same time, he demonized, albeit somewhat mildly, the gay and lesbian community in Colorado by evincing a portrait of them as a powerful minority attempting to privilege its point of view via intrusive and morally questionable laws, which Scalia later referred to as "preferential" (p. 638). He implied that this was surely unreasonable and should not be countenanced—that the Justices cannot allow a deviant minority to impose its will on the reasonable and victimized heterosexual majority, be they in Colorado or anywhere else. However, he did not argue, in the manner of Justice Burger, that consensual, adult gay sex in private is worse than rape, nor did he assert that there is an utter divide between gays and family, as did Justice White. In this comparative sense, anyway, Scalia's denunciation of gay identity is positively civilized and restrained.

Scalia did argue in his dissent that, just as the state may declare as reprehensible certain conduct—"murder, for example, or polygamy, or cruelty to animals," so should it be able to prevent gays and lesbians from obtaining protective antidiscrimination laws (*Romer v. Evans,* 1996, p. 644). For example, he wrote that "the Court's disposition today suggests that these provisions are unconstitutional and that polygamy must be permitted in these states . . . unless, of course, polygamists for some reason have fewer constitutional rights than homosexuals" (p. 648). Scalia's denigrative use of sarcasm in this statement is obvious, and yet, while he clearly demonstrated serious disrespect for gay and lesbian identity, he did not go as far as Burger and White did in *Bowers.* On the other hand, Scalia equated gays and lesbians with not just polygamists, but also with murderers and those who are cruel to animals. So, while Scalia's condemnation may have been less severe than that meted out by Justices White and Burger in *Bowers*, it appears that this difference is one of degree rather than of kind. I still cling, however precariously, to the claim that Scalia's dissent in *Romer* represents a form of progress over the stigmatic rhetoric articulated in *Bowers*. At a minimum, I believe it is significant that the negative imagery conjured up in these two cases migrated from a majority opinion in 1986 to a three-person dissent in 1996.

Justice Scalia was willing to engage the moral issues that frame the debate over gay and lesbian civil rights. Conversely, the majority opinion in *Romer*, while implicitly pro-gay/lesbian civil rights, did not make the explicit moral case for such a stance. Instead, the majority engaged in an abstract discussion of how the Fourteenth Amendment to the Constitution applies to Amendment 2. As Halley (1997) has argued, "[Scalia] at least reminds us that Amendment 2 involves our passions . . . the majority Justices, on the other hand, present a bland, apersonal, almost faceless speaker" (p. 437). Halley believes that this case is about differing moral visions, and she wants the Court to address this explicitly.

I assert that the shift in negative identity construction from 1986 to 1996, by those on the Court who are hostile to the gay and lesbian community, represents real social and legal change. That is, if one believes that gays, lesbians, and bisexuals should be adjudged the moral equals of heterosexuals, and if one even minimally endorses the gay and lesbian civil rights agenda, then the observable reduction in the Court's open and vigorous hostility toward homosexual subjects represents progress, albeit on a rather modest scale. However, I must also note that the collective identity constructed by White, Burger, and Scalia cannot but do harm to gays and lesbians in their broader struggle to achieve full and equal citizenship in the United States. This is true whether that rhetoric is explicit and extreme, or more implicit and subtle. In any event, the shift that occurred between these two cases is to be applauded.

Positive Endorsement

One can also find in the law images of gay and lesbian subjects that recognize their essential humanity and demonstrate an awareness of the reality of their lives. Perhaps the best known of these depictions can be found in Justice Blackmun's dissenting opinion in *Bowers*. Quoting from *Paris Adult Theatre I v. Slaton* (1973), Blackmun argued that sexual intimacy between consenting adults in the privacy of their bedrooms (including same-sex couples) is "a sensitive, key relationship of human existence, central to family life, community welfare, and the development of human personality" (p. 63). Implicitly, Blackmun reconnected gay and lesbian individuals with the key institutions of family and community, and made it clear that they lead multifaceted and complex lives, although he did not elaborate on this critical theme. In fact, the primary emphasis in Blackmun's dissent is on the freedom that individuals should have to choose "the form and nature of . . . intensely personal bonds" with other consenting adults (*Bowers v. Hardwick,* 1986, p. 205). Nevertheless, Blackmun did articulate a gay and lesbian identity that in no way precludes a strong connection to family and community.

Sandel (1989) has argued that Justice Blackmun's dissent, while in many ways entirely commendable, places too much emphasis on toleration and not enough on "the moral permissibility of the practices at issue" (p. 537). Sandel believes that courts must begin to openly and forcefully defend the morality of gay and lesbian citizens if the gay civil rights movement is to make progress in the long run. I argue that Sandel's analysis of Blackmun's opinion is only partially correct, since he fails to recognize that Blackmun's valuation of gay identity is integral to both family and community. Although it is certainly true that there were definite limits to Blackmun's willingness to define fully the positive aspects of gay identity, the case can be made that Blackmun did engage in a form, however limited, of affirmational rhetoric.

Ortiz (1993) argues that Blackmun's dissent in *Bowers* offered only "a very thin, unthreatening and largely desexualized description of gay identity" (p. 1851). Ortiz believes, however, that Blackmun's avoidance of a dense description of gay identity provides space within which the gay and lesbian community can define themselves collectively. According to Ortiz, the relatively neutral approach adopted by Blackmun may prove to be politically effective at a time when society is just beginning to move away from the sort of thick[4] negative descriptions of gay identity offered up by Justices White and Burger in *Bowers*. However, Ortiz also suggests that, at some point in the future, "for the purpose of . . . empowering the group, new and positive thick master descriptions may serve even better" (p. 1856). From Ortiz's perspective, then, Blackmun's dissent represents not the positive endorsement of gay and lesbian identity that I argue it represents, but rather a version of identity neutrality that gives to gays themselves the power of self-definition.

An example of the legal construction of a reasonably positive and full-bodied description of gay identity by a court can be found in the case of *Watkins v. United States Army* (1988). This case was initially decided on appeal by a three-judge panel of the Ninth Circuit Court of Appeals. By a vote of 2 to 1, this panel ruled that the military's policy of excluding gay and lesbian personnel violated the Fourteenth Amendment's Equal Protection Clause. This broad decision was dramatically narrowed upon appeal to the entire Ninth Circuit Court of Appeals; the ruling upheld the reinstatement of Perry Watkins, an openly gay member of the military, but did so on narrow technical grounds.

The two judges who struck down the military's anti-gay policy (instituted in 1981 under the leadership of President Ronald Reagan) began their opinion by noting that the Army itself consistently gave Mr. Watkins high-grade evaluations throughout his military career. Judge Norris, author of the majority opinion, highlighted the following evaluations of Watkins by several of his superiors:

> Watkins is without exception, one of the finest . . . Supervisors I have encountered . . . [his] duty performance has been outstanding in every regard . . . Watkins' potential is unlimited . . . the best clerk I have known . . . [he did] a fantastic job—excellent. . . . From daily personal contacts I can attest to the outstanding professional attitude, integrity, and suitability for assignment [to a Nuclear project requiring security clearance]. . . . He has, in fact, become one of our most respected and trusted soldiers, both by his superiors and subordinates. . . . Watkins' duty performance has been outstanding in every regard. . . . I would gladly welcome another opportunity to serve with him, and firmly believe that he will be an asset to

any unit to which he is assigned. (*Watkins v. United States Army*, 1988, pp. 1430-1432)

Here, then, is a thick description of gay conduct that offers a startling contrast to that offered by Justices White and Burger in *Bowers*. Judge Norris draws the sort of detailed and complex portrait of gay identity that Justice Blackmun only hinted at in his dissent in *Bowers*. It is this kind of construction of gay identity that is so necessary to progressive social change. That is, as per Sandel's (1989) argument, unless the courts challenge "adverse views of homosexuality itself," even legal victories are "unlikely to win for homosexuals more than a thin and fragile toleration" (p. 537). I do not think it is important, or even reasonable, for judges to attach positive qualities to individuals based solely on their sexual orientation; however, I think it is vitally important for them to be willing to acknowledge both the good and the bad that attach to all individuals, regardless of their sexual orientation. Judge Norris made just this argument in *Watkins* (1988) when he asserted the "irrelevance of sexual orientation to the quality of a person's contribution to society" (p. 1445). Was exemplary service driven by Watkins' gay identity? Probably not, but his gay identity also did not preclude such service as an officer in the United States armed forces.

Judge Norris placed at the heart of his analysis a consideration of whether homosexuals constitute a *suspect class* under the terms of the Fourteenth Amendment's Equal Protection Clause. The best example of a suspect class is that of race—that is, if the government promulgates a policy that uses race as a relevant category (as when the government directed that Japanese Americans be relocated to camps in the western deserts during World War II), then the courts will look with great skepticism at the constitutionality of such a policy. If homosexuals do constitute a suspect class, the courts will examine any government policies using sexual orientation as a category with *strict scrutiny*, which means that the government must demonstrate that any policy singling out this class of citizens must advance a compelling government interest as narrowly as possible. Judge Norris emphasized in the court's majority opinion the military's focus on sexual orientation rather than on sexual conduct. Judge Norris noted that "the ultimate evidentiary issue is whether he or she has a homosexual orientation" (*Watkins v. United States Army*, 1988, p. 1436). This point was made throughout Norris' opinion, and he implied repeatedly that, if the military simply forbade homosexual sex by its members, whether with civilians or other members of the military, then the policy would be beyond legal reproach. I argue that this key point indicates the willingness of even a relatively progressive judge to erase a part of gay and lesbian identity *in pursuit of fair treatment based on sexual orientation*, and that this erasure implies the rejection of a significant part of what it means to be gay.

In trying to determine if sexual orientation constitutes a suspect class, Judge Norris had to consider whether "discrimination embodies a gross unfairness that is sufficiently inconsistent with the ideals of equal protection to term it invidious" (*Watkins v. United States Army*, 1988, p. 1444). Judge Norris held that discrimination against gay and lesbian members of the military meets this standard. He argued that "classifications based on sexual orientation reflect prejudice and inaccurate stereotypes" (p. 1445). The court thus emphasized not only a relatively thick description of real gay people, but also an explicit repudiation of the profoundly negative portraits of gay individuals drawn by the military and other institutions that use sexual orientation to shape their policies.

In *Watkins* and the dissent in *Bowers*, one can see, within the limits I've noted, a positive complex identity set forth in legal discourse. In contrast with the negative rhetoric articulated by such Justices as Burger, White, and Scalia, the jurists in each of these cases provided respect for, and appreciation of, the lives of gay citizens through legal endorsement. And while neither Blackmun nor Norris provide an ideal form of affirmational rhetoric, they nevertheless did a better job than the other judges analyzed in this chapter. An alternative to these two models, suggested by Daniel Ortiz with regard to Blackmun's dissent in Bowers, is sketched out below.

Legal Neutrality

The Supreme Court of Wisconsin, in *Holtzman v. Knott* (1995), grappled with the issue of same-sex couples and visitation rights involving children. Ms. Holtzman and Ms. Knott had been involved in a relationship for over ten years. Ms. Knott was artificially inseminated and bore a child during the fifth year of their union. Five years later, the relationship between the two women ended, and Ms. Knott took the child to live with her. Ms. Knott eventually denied visitation rights to Ms. Holtzman, whereupon Ms. Holtzman went to a state circuit court to enforce such rights. The trial court held that Wisconsin's family law did not protect nontraditional families with regard to visitation rights and that Ms. Holtzmann had no legal recourse. The case was then appealed to the Wisconsin Supreme Court, which held, by a vote of 4 to 3, that state trial courts could, if they so chose, enforce child visitation rights in the context of same-sex couples.

Justice Shirley Abrahamson, writing for the Court, reasoned that while Wisconsin state law does not explicitly recognize nontraditional relationships, it also does not specifically deny visitation rights in cases involving same-sex couples. This legislative silence, Abrahamson decided, allows the courts, under their established equitable right to protect the best interests of children in dissolved relationships, to order visitation rights. State trial courts, therefore, have the *option* of ordering visitation rights in cases involving same-sex couples. To trigger such court involvement, the petitioning parent must meet various standards of proof. The relevant burdens regarding proof are as follows: first, the biological or adopted parent must have agreed to, and fostered, a parentlike relationship between the child and the petitioning parent. Second, the petitioner must have assumed parenthood by "taking significant responsibility for the child's care, education, and development" (*Holtzman v. Knott*, 1995, p. 695). Third, the petitioner must have established over time a "bonded, dependent relationship parental in nature" with the child in question (p. 695). Abrahamson made it clear that the context for each of these considerations must always be the best interests of the child.

The Wisconsin Supreme Court approached the issue of gay and lesbian identity with studious neutrality. That is, Justice Abrahamson constructed neither a positive nor a negative portrait of gay people. Rather, she provided for homosexuals the opportunity to make their case for visitation rights to a state trial court. It is important to note that Abrahamson did provide for gays a legal space within which they have the chance to establish an identity as parents worthy of being granted visitation rights. In this sense, members of the gay and lesbian communities were empowered to define themselves to others. At the same time, however, it is discouraging to note that gay and lesbian parents seeking visitation rights must essentially make a plea to a court in order to establish their parent-like relationship to their child or children. Heterosexual parents seeking visitation rights need not make such a plea—their status as parents to their children is taken for granted by the Wisconsin courts. It is also worth noting that it is likely that many trial courts in Wisconsin, particularly those in the more rural northern and western counties, are unlikely to be convinced by *any* gay parent that he or she deserves visitation rights. In other words, the self-defined gay identity provided for by Justice Abrahamson is subject to emphatic rejection by trial judges committed to a negative and stereotypical view of homosexuals. Conversely, of course, at least some trial judges may give a fair hearing to gay and lesbian parents.

The U.S. Supreme Court's decision in *Romer v. Evans* (1996) involved an amendment to the Colorado state constitution. This amendment, Amendment 2, was passed by popular referendum in 1992. Amendment 2 prohibited the passing of local legislation to protect gay and lesbian citizens from discrimination in employment, housing, public accommodations, and health and welfare services. As Justice Kennedy noted in his majority opinion, Amendment 2 would have gone even further, for it "prohibits all legislative, executive or judicial action at any level of state or local government designed to protect" those of gay, lesbian, or bisexual orientation (*Romer v. Evans*, 1996, p. 624). This statewide referendum was largely a response to the passage of local laws forbidding discrimination based on sexual orientation in cities such as Denver, Aspen, and Boulder. The Court viewed Amendment 2 as being in violation of the U.S. Constitution's Fourteenth Amendment, which requires that a state provide equal protection of the law to all its citizens, and struck it down by a vote of 6 to 3.

Justice Kennedy's majority opinion took no position on the morality of gay, lesbian, and bisexual identity. Rather, Kennedy spoke in the abstract terms of equal protection doctrine and of those classes of citizens who fit within the umbrella of this protective amendment. This is in sharp contrast to the rhetoric employed by Justice Scalia in his dissent, whereby the presumed immorality of gay and lesbian subjects is articulated, albeit in indirect fashion. As Halley (1997) notes, *Romer* "interrupts [Scalia's] vituperative call to homosexual readers, implicitly promising them that the Supreme Court can address them in the register of cool, objective reason, as persons with personhood" (p. 435). The majority thus sidestep the moral case that can be made on behalf of gay and lesbian citizens, preferring instead to assume a more neutral stance regarding the identity of this group.

Justice Kennedy emphasized the fact that Amendment 2 would shut an entire class of citizens out of the political process: it would prevent them from seeking, at either the state or local level, antidiscrimination legislation. He argued it would deny the most fundamental right to engage in the political process of lawmaking to gay, lesbian, and bisexual citizens. Thus, the Fourteenth Amendment's Equal Protection Clause conflicts with Amendment 2. Gay citizens, he concluded, must have at least the opportunity to lobby for protective laws. The state may not foreclose such political activity prematurely. Kennedy argued that the law should be impartial in its treatment of Colorado citizens, and that gays and lesbians are as deserving of the procedural protection as are any other group of citizens. He also argued that Amendment 2 does not bear a rational relationship to a legitimate state interest. Rather, Amendment 2 merely expresses animosity toward an unpopular group. As such, "it is a status-based enactment divorced from any factual context from which we could discern a relationship to legitimate state interests" (*Romer v. Evans,* 1996, p. 632).

One could argue that the Court's majority opinion in *Romer* does present an implicitly positive portrait of gay and lesbian citizens. First, the Court argued that gays and lesbians cannot be singled out, relative to heterosexuals, for exclusion from local political struggles to secure their group-based interests. They share with mainstream heterosexuals, then, the status of citizens deserving of equal protection of state law. Second, the Court openly branded those who supported Amendment 2 as the perpetrators of invidious discrimination against a group of citizens who have not given cause for this animosity. As such, the opponents of gay and lesbian civil rights are branded as the deviant and despised group, while the gay and lesbian community is, at least implicitly, seen as the innocent victims of irrational homophobia. However, I argue that, while both of these arguments have some persuasive power, the Court ultimately undermined the construction of a positive gay and lesbian identity by using either negative terms (as when gays and lesbians are defined as innocent victims who are positive only in the sense that they *lack* a negative identity) or masked terms (as when they are presumed to possess the same rights of citizenship as heterosexuals). The Court's lines of argument, while laudable, do not rise to quite the same level of affirmational rhetoric as Blackmun's dissent in *Bowers* or Judge Norris' majority opinion in *Watkins*.

What I think is most notable about Justice Kennedy's opinion in *Romer* is his condemnation of those Coloradans who voted for Amendment 2. Kennedy made it clear that, in the Court's view, those who favored this referendum were not pursuing a legitimate state interest, but instead merely sought to express their animosity toward a traditionally reviled group of citizens. The tables have indeed been turned; the Court in *Romer* makes no bones about taking to task those who oppose antidiscrimination laws that protect gay and lesbian citizens. Those who are, in the words of one scholar, "homoprejudicial," are thus placed in a defensive position (Logan, 1996). Conversely, in *Bowers* it was indisputably the anti-gay rights advocates who were on the offensive, with the Court's hearty support, and we see a modest attempt to defend the gay rights position in Blackmun's dissent. Without a doubt, then, both society and the courts have shifted their positions between 1986 and 1996. What a difference a decade makes!

Robert Nagel, a conservative legal scholar, takes extreme exception to this turnabout in *Romer*. He argues that the people of Colorado, in passing Amendment 2, were merely "playing defense" (Nagel, 1997, p. 167). More specifically, Nagel believes that the impetus behind the referendum in Colorado was not animosity, but rather an "effort to protect [a] way of life . . . [through a] touchingly innocent American commitment to legalism" (p. 188), and he threatens that one can only wonder what (presumably heterosexual) people who "feel increasingly frightened, isolated, and unable to shape their lives . . . will do if their native faith in legalistic defenses is destroyed" (pp. 188-189). Regardless of how one interprets this legal and social shift, however, it seems clear that the array of social and argumentative forces both reflected and expressed in *Bowers* had indeed shifted substantially by 1996.

CONCLUSIONS

Kenneth Karst (1995) points out that many queer theorists argue that "sexual orientation identity . . . is mythical" and fails to capture the intense diversity and individuality of those identified as gay (p. 309). This postmodern critique of the case for gay and lesbian identity, while in some ways quite meritorious, seems both socially and politically dangerous. Karst himself makes a similar point when he argues that human societies cannot function effectively without various categories of group identity. Such identities, Karst emphasizes, allow us, as human beings, to make some sense out of an infinitely complex social world and to take some sort of concerted action based on those identities. Realistically, I think the question becomes one of determining what collective identity is either assigned to, or expressed by, gay and lesbian individuals in the United States. It is ultimately impossible for the courts, or anyone else, to wholly determine the identity of any person or group of people because the human experience is simply too shifting, complex, and ineffably multifaceted; however, within these sorts of bounded possibilities, I do think it important to determine how the courts have attempted to collectively identify gay and lesbian subjects.

I have analyzed in this chapter the roles the law has played, and perhaps should play, in the construction of gay identity in the late twentieth century. Certainly it is clear that the profoundly negative descriptions of homosexuals set forth by the Supreme Court in *Bowers* can only contribute to society's condemnation of gays and lesbians and, relatedly, impede the gay/lesbian civil rights movement. The legalized homoprejudice penned by Justices White and Burger must be contested, and contested vigorously, by the gay, lesbian, and bisexual communities and their allies if we are to move in the direction of progressive social change regarding sexual orientation. An encouraging development is the more restrained condemnation of gay and lesbian identity found in Scalia's opinion in

Romer. Progress can also be seen in the fact that this condemnation switched from the majority in *Bowers* to the dissent in *Romer*. On the other hand, this more subtle form of gay bashing may prove to be harder to combat, since Scalia's relatively sophisticated attack on the gay and lesbian community doesn't have the same harsh ring as the rather crude stereotypes invoked by Justices Burger and White in *Bowers*.

The more complex and positive portraits of gay people painted in Blackmun's dissent in *Bowers* and in Judge Norris' majority opinion in *Watkins* serve as models, albeit significantly flawed, of how the law might begin to construct an ideology of sexual orientation that will further the cause of gay civil rights. Given the tentative and somewhat limited endorsement of homosexuals in these relatively progressive opinions, however, it may be that the relative neutrality offered by Justice Abrahamson in *Holtzman* is the most promising form of legal ideology for the combined gay and lesbian community at this particular moment. At the same time, it must be noted that, although Abrahamson does give gay parents the opportunity to tell their own stories, too much discretionary authority is vested in state trial court judges who may choose to reject the self-identification of these petitioners.

Perhaps the most prevalent legal model in the 1990s has been that of legal neutrality. I argue that this model prevails in Abrahamson's majority opinion in *Holtzman* and in Kennedy's majority opinion in *Romer*. This approach seems most consonant with the mainstream view of courts as neutral referees in political struggles that must take place within a constitutional framework requiring equal protection of the laws and a measure of individual privacy from oppressive government intervention. Such a judicial stance can provide for gays, lesbians, and bisexuals the chance to define themselves without interference from self-anointed moral guardians. This form of legal neutrality may, as Ortiz (1993) argues, be the best approach at this point in time. Rush (1997) believes that "the ability to self-define is liberating and empowering" (p. 97). Similarly, Danielsen (1995) places faith in "the ways in which legal discourse . . . might be able to provide the space for our complexity and differentness to be represented but not determined" (p. 58). Finally, in the view of Jacobs (1993), given the fact that "moral disapproval for homosexuality has remained constant" since about 1970, while political tolerance for a range of gay rights positions has increased significantly,[5] perhaps it makes sense to "shift gay rights discourse from moral language . . . toward political language" (p. 754).

I believe that, in the not too distant future, more courts will begin to provide positive, relatively thick descriptions of gay identity that reflect that community's own narratives and experiences as complex human beings worthy of full citizenship. And this shift will both express and reinforce society's understanding of gay identity. We need to press, then, for a legal and social discourse that empowers the gay, lesbian, and bisexual communities and makes a positive contribution to progressive social change at the level of social perceptions of what it means to be gay, lesbian, or bisexual. At the same time, as Jacobs (1993) argues, a rhetoric of tolerance may be more likely to be effective at present. But, if this is the approach that the courts take, then one must understand that "the protective rhetoric and policies of tolerance can be appropriately understood as a way station en route to rhetoric and policies which embrace and affirm" (p. 755). Additionally, I think it is critical that the gay community and its allies seize on the current legal and social climate of political tolerance to articulate a gay and lesbian perspective that paves the way for more affirmational legal and social discourse on identity.

NOTES

1. *Eisenstadt v. Baird* (1972) validated the right of unmarried persons to gain access to birth control.

2. In *Roe v. Wade* (1973) the Court upheld the right of pregnant women, married or not, to have access to abortion, with the support of a licensed physician, prior to fetal viability.

3. *Griswold v. Connecticut* (1965) was the Court's first attempt to define concretely the privacy rights created by the Bill of Right's first eight amendments and the Fourteenth Amendment. These rights were extended initially to married couples seeking birth control devices.

4. "Thick description" is a term coined by Geertz (1973), an anthropologist. Geertz used this term to evince how he believes we can best understand human society—by providing dense, detailed narratives that emphasize the concrete realities of everyday life, rather than abstract theories.

5. A Gallup Poll, conducted in 1997, found that roughly 84 percent of Americans believe that homosexuals should have equal job opportunities (up from 56 percent in 1977), while 59 percent still believe that homosexuality is morally wrong (Berke, 1998).

REFERENCES

Aristotle. (1943). *Aristotle's politics* (B. Jowett, Trans.). New York: The Modern Library.

Berke, R. (1998, August 2). Chasing the polls on gay rights. *The New York Times,* sec. 4, p. 3.

Boswell, J. (1980). *Christianity, social tolerance, and homosexuality.* Chicago, IL: University of Chicago Press.

Bowers v. Hardwick, 478 U.S. 186 (1986).

Brown v. Board of Education, 349 U.S. 483 (1954).

Butler, C. J. (1998). The Defense of Marriage Act: Congress's use of narrative in the debate over same-sex marriage. *New York University Law Review, 73*(3), 841-879.

Chauncey, G., Duberman, M., and Vicinus, M. (Eds.). (1989). *Hidden from history: Reclaiming the gay and lesbian past.* New York: New American Library.

Coombs, M. (1996). Comment: between women/between men: The significance for lesbianism of historical understandings of same-(male)sex sexual activities. *Yale Journal of Law and the Humanities, 8*(1), 241-261.

Cruikshank, M. (1992). *The gay and lesbian liberation movement.* New York: Routledge.

Danielsen, D. (1995). Identity strategies: Representing pregnancy and homosexuality. In D. Danielsen and K. Engle (Eds.), *After identity: A reader in law and culture* (pp. 39-61). New York: Routledge.

D'Augelli, A. R. (1998). Developmental implications of victimization of lesbian, gay, and bisexual youths. In G. M. Herek (Ed.), *Psychological perspectives on lesbian and gay issues: Volume 4. Stigma and sexual orientation: Understanding prejudice against lesbian, gay men, and bisexuals* (pp. 187-210). Thousand Oaks, CA: Sage.

Dennis v. United States, 341 U.S. 494 (1951).

Eisenstadt v. Baird, 405 U.S. 438 (1972).

Foster, S. R. (1998). The symbolism of rights and the costs of symbolism: Some thoughts on the campaign for same-sex marriage. *Temple Political and Civil Rights Law Review, 7*(2), 319-328.

Gagnier, R. (1990). Feminist postmodernism: The end of feminism or the ends of theory? In D. Rhode (Ed.), *Theoretical perspectives on sexual difference,* (pp. 21-30). New Haven, CT: Yale University Press.

Geertz, C. (1973). *The interpretation of cultures.* New York: Basic Books.

Griswold v. Connecticut, 381 U.S. 479 (1965).

Halley, J. E. (1997). *Romer v. Hardwick. University of Colorado Law Review, 68*(2), 429-452.

Holtzman v. Knott, 193 Wis.2d 649 (1995).

Jacobs, A. M. (1993). The rhetorical construction of rights: The case of the gay rights movement, 1969-1991. *Nebraska Law Review, 72*(3), 723-759.

Karst, K. (1995). Myths of identity: Individual and group portraits of race and sexual orientation. *UCLA Law Review, 43*(2), 263-369.

Korematsu v. United States, 323 U.S. 214 (1944).

Logan, C. R. (1996). Homophobia? No, homoprejudice. *Journal of Homosexuality, 31*(3), 31-53.

Mohr, R. D. (1988). *Gays/Justice: A study of ethics, society, and law.* New York: Columbia University Press.

Nagel, R. F. (1997). Playing defense. *William and Mary Bill of Rights Journal, 6*(1), 167-199.

Nava, M. and Dawidoff, R. (1994). *Created equal: Why gay rights matter to America.* New York: St. Martin's Press.

Ortiz, D. (1993). Creating controversy: Essentialism and constructivism and the politics of gay identity. *Virginia Law Review, 79*(7), 1833-1857.

Paris Adult Theatre I v. Slaton, 413 U.S. 49 (1973).

Roe v. Wade, 410 U.S. 113 (1973).

Romer v. Evans, 517 U.S. 620 (1996).

Rush, S. E. (1997). Equal protection analogies—Identity and "passing": Race and sexual orientation. *Harvard BlackLetter Law Journal, 13*, 65-106.

Sandel, M. (1989). Moral argument and liberal toleration: Abortion and homosexuality. *California Law Review, 77*(3), 521-538.

Tocqueville, Alexis de (1835/1948). *Democracy in America*, P. Bradley (Ed.). New York: Alfred A. Knopf, p. 280.

Watkins v. United States Army, 837 F.2d. 1428 (1988).

Chapter 3

Homophobia in Academia: Examination and Critique

Linda Gannon

Although lesbians and gay men represent a sizable minority in most cultures and in spite of recent activism in Western cultures, lesbians and gay men continue to experience social and economic oppression. The discrimination against and oppression of lesbians and gay men are different from other prejudicial attitudes and behaviors in terms of origins and construction: the target of homosexual prejudice is behavior and/or worldview rather than skin color, ethnicity, or ancestry—the more common sources of prejudice; furthermore, while sexism and racism date back through history (5,000 years for sexism), prejudice against those whose choice of intimate partner is a person of the same sex is a relatively recent phenomenon; and, finally, some of the more insidious forms of the oppression are based on an assumption that homosexuality is, in some way, contagious—that is, learning about homosexuality or working with a homosexual will somehow cause one to "catch" it. Yet, the manifestations and consequences of prejudice against women, racial and ethnic minorities, and gay men and lesbians share common ground. The oppressed individuals are frequently blamed for social problems such as drug addiction, child abuse, and sexually transmitted diseases; they experience discrimination in the areas of housing, employment, insurance, health care, and education; their "dif-

The author would like to thank Jill Stevens, George Moskos, and Robert Cerchio for their substantive contributions to this chapter; and Lynn Pardie, Tracy Luchetta, George Moskos, and Jill Stevens for their comments and editorial help.

43

ferences" are exaggerated; and justifications for the discrimination are often couched in terms of biological reductionism.

The history of homophobia is an interesting one. In ancient Greece, homosexual behavior, at least among men, was expected and culturally normal. With the emergence of Christianity, although homosexual behavior came to be labeled a sin and/or a crime (as was adultery), such behavior did not confer an identity. In the nineteenth century, romantic and intimate relationships between persons of the same sex were common, accepted, and were not associated with a stigmatizing label. By the end of the nineteenth century, Freudian theory (which emphasized sexuality) and Darwinian theory (which emphasized procreation) dominated Western thought. Sexuality came to be seen as a central force of personality and as the prime motivator of behavior. The overwhelming influence of medicine and science during the twentieth century demanded that "normality" be explicitly defined and that any person who did not strictly adhere to this definition be categorized as ill. In this way, homosexuality was labeled pathological. The desire of the medical community for increased credibility and power motivated the development of cures and, thus, biological and behavioral "cures" of homosexuality became popular in the 1950s and 1960s (Bohan, 1996).

During this time, psychology developed as both a clinical and a research discipline. As clinicians, psychologists accepted (often unwillingly) the nosology of medicine wherein homosexuality was defined as an illness. However, as scholars, they were unable to document adjustment problems or personality pathology related solely to homosexuality. Equally crucial was the overwhelming research evidence that the "cures" were uniquely unsuccessful in transforming homosexuals into heterosexuals. By the 1970s, the medical community could no longer ignore the mounting evidence, and homosexuality was no longer "officially" considered a pathology. Since the 1970s, not only have many in the field of psychology worked to eradicate the view that homosexuality is pathological but, in fact, have advocated accepting homosexuality as a cultural norm. This has not been readily accomplished. The culture has internalized the pathological designation for homosexuals and, consequently, has provided powerful extremist groups, such as the anti-communism movement of the 1950s and the religious right movement of the 1980s, with a scapegoat for "evil" and social deterioration.

Although the history of homophobia provides a logical background for present-day prejudice, the intensity and pervasiveness of the prejudice against gay men and lesbians seems of greater magnitude than that which might result from a briefly defined psychiatric disorder. Indeed, a major conundrum of homophobia is the source of it. Homophobia is frequently attributed to fundamentalist religious beliefs. Yet, many forms of sexual behavior are labeled as sinful according to various religious doctrines but are not the focus of widespread discrimination and oppression. Persons who adhere to Catholicism and who divorce and remarry may be censured, they may lose a few friends, but they do not lose their jobs, they are not violently attacked, they are not evicted from their housing. Others attribute homophobia to beliefs that homosexuality is not "natural." Yet, however one defines "natural," homosexuality is surely not less natural than breast implants, a football game, celibacy, owning fifty cats, or wearing spike heels; yet, these "unnatural" behaviors are not sources of prejudice and discrimination. Finally, some homophobic persons endorse negative stereotypes that homosexuals are dangerous and subversive—that they are pedophiles, that they recruit children to their lifestyle, that they are promiscuous, and that they hate persons of the opposite sex. Although such myths have been frequently and convincingly dispelled in scholarly work and the popular media, homophobia continues. Thus, a motivation for gathering the information presented in this chapter has been to explore the reasons for the prejudice against lesbians and gay men.

PARTNER BENEFITS IN ACADEMIA

Academia has historically been a primary source for the initiation and proliferation of liberal attitudes. Explicit policies aimed at ending discrimination against women and racial minorities and, more recently, against lesbians and gay men, have often originated in institutions of higher learning. Today, some institutions, corporations, and government agencies have affirmative action policies and educational guidelines which state that they do not discriminate on the basis of race, sex, or sexual orientation. Although such policies are necessary to the goal of ending unfair work and educational practices, activists have long recognized the inadequacy of simple nondiscrimination polices. While these may provide equal access (if sincere), other changes and modifications are required to ensure social, economic, and political equality. For example, many academic institutions have recognized the necessity of providing adequate and accessible day care in order to recruit and retain qualified women employees and students. Similarly, a university may sincerely attempt to recruit African-American applicants, but ignore a prejudicial, segregated community and neglect racism in course content and extracurricular activities.

Policies stating that hiring or promotion will not be influenced by sexual orientation are a step toward attracting and retaining gay men and lesbians as faculty, administrators, and students but will prove inadequate without additional support. Since most states do not yet legally recognize marriage between two people of the same sex and since marriage is currently regarded as the legal state of social partnership, lesbians and gay men are not "equal" to heterosexuals with regard to health insurance, housing allowances, and access to educational and recreational facilities for partners and families of employees. Providing partner benefits at institutions of higher learning would attract highly qualified employees who happen to be gay men or lesbians. University communities in which gay men and lesbians participate fully provide models of respect and equality which other communities and work environments can emulate. Lesbian and gay academics are also excellent resources for heterosexual faculty who wish to eliminate heterosexist bias from their teaching and research. Moreover, the developmental state of most undergraduates is characterized by openness to new ideas, attitudes, and behaviors which makes it a crucial life stage for gay and lesbian students to develop positive self-concepts, and for heterosexual students to develop goals of social and political justice and personal appreciation for those different from themselves. Although policies of universities and colleges directly impact only a small percentage of the population, these institutions are generally considered to be our cultural and philosophical leaders. As such, they can be highly influential by creating fair and just models. As of 1994, approximately thirty colleges and professional schools and twenty non-profit organizations offer domestic partner benefits to their employees (Zuckerman and Simons, 1994). As of 1997, forty-one cities, twelve counties, and four states as well as about 10 percent of all U.S. companies offer such benefits (*Human Rights Campaign Quarterly*, 1997).

I conducted in-depth interviews with leaders of two successful movements to institute partner benefits for gay men and lesbian employees in two academic settings in the United States: a small elite and private undergraduate liberal arts college in the east, and a large public research university in the rural midwest. My goals are to elucidate situations, strategies, and policies that have been supportive or obstructive of changes and to understand the sources of homophobia as expressed in these contexts.

Similarities between the two institutions included having recognized and long-standing (at least twenty-five years) undergraduate organizations for lesbians and gay men and, more recently (since 1990), the formation of faculty/staff organizations working for partner benefits. At both institutions, these organizations work to incorporate lesbian and gay issues into the curriculum and to provide a welcoming and supportive environment for gay men and lesbian employees and students. There are, however, important differences between the institutions. At the public university, the employee organization includes anyone interested in working on the goals; it is a grass-roots organization and somewhat invisible since it lacks institutional legitimacy. At the private college, a substantial endowment from an alumnus was targeted to create a small select committee of students, staff, and faculty with the directive to eliminate homophobia; the committee had considerable resources available and institutional recognition. Leaders at both schools reported administrative support. However, at the public university, the support was quiet and reactive whereas, at the private college, the support was visible, public, and proactive. At the close of negotiations, the public university announced the new policy in memos to department chairs and deans—there was no public announcement. In contrast, the private college was disappointed by the lack of national media attention. The gaining of partner benefits at the public university was not associated with an obvious change in "atmosphere" for gay men and lesbians; at the private college, a recent job description specified "expertise in lesbian/gay studies" and five courses on gay and lesbian issues have been developed.

Another major difference between the institutions is in their definition of partner benefits. At the private college, partner benefits are defined as being identical to those available to opposite-sex spouses and include health and life insurance, family sick leave, housing allowances, travel allowances, and use of college facilities. At the public university, partner benefits are defined as a "spouse card" allowing the partner to use the recreation center and library as well as to attend university events at a reduced cost—benefits more symbolic than real, perhaps, but important nonetheless. The limited benefits at the public university were rationalized on the basis that other benefits (e.g., health insurance) require legislative approval and would apply to all state funded institutions of higher learning. While members of the administration at the public university were supportive of providing the limited benefits (spouse card), they were not enthusiastic about lobbying the legislature. Consequently, there is currently an effort to form a state-wide advocacy coalition in order to obtain complete partner benefits at all state-supported schools.

Insight into the sources and expressions of homophobia can be gleaned by examining the criteria for being a designated or "legitimate" partner. These included:

1. Declaration of same-sex partnership (signatures)
2. Possession of joint mortgage or lease
3. Designation of partner as life insurance beneficiary
4. Designation of partner as beneficiary in will
5. Joint ownership of durable property and health care powers of attorney
6. Joint ownership of a motor vehicle
7. Joint checking account
8. Partnership duration of at least three years
9. Stated intention to spend the rest of their lives together

At the public university, partners were required to satisfy three of Criteria 1 through 7 and, at the private college, Criteria 1, 8, and 9 were required. As is obvious, at both schools, same-sex partners were required to satisfy more stringent criteria than opposite-sex spouses. Because objections were made publicly and formally at the private college and quietly at the public university, in practice, only Criterion 1 is required at either institution. However, the criteria reveal a primary focus of the negative stereotype of the homosexual—that homosexuals are sexually promiscuous and do not form "serious" long-term relationships.

Discussion

Economic factors are often believed to underlie sexism and racism; that is, equal access to employment by minority races and/or women would result in fewer jobs and less money available for white men. While monetary concerns have not been emphasized as a source of homosexual prejudice, concern with material resources are subtly woven into the process of obtaining partner benefits. First, the reader might note the criteria for partner legitimacy outlined previously; six of the nine criteria require that the participating parties officially combine their money and property—an odd way to define an intimate and lasting emotional relationship. Second, both institutions of higher education were, to some extent, driven in their negotiations by monetary concerns. At the private college, the drive for partner benefits was initiated as part of a comprehensive campaign to eliminate homophobia on the campus, and this campaign was the result of a substantial endowment designated for that purpose. We cannot predict what current policies and attitudes would exist today without the endowment. At the public university, the administration agreed at once to the demands of the committee for a "spouse card." This ready accession was interpreted by the committee as a reflection of the administration's fear that not acceding would generate unwanted publicity from protests and demonstrations on the campus. The administration did not make a public announcement when this benefit was approved, which supports this interpretation. The clear desire not to alert the public was, at least partially, motivated by the recognition that the public pays the bills.

At publicly funded schools, the primary excuse for not granting full partner benefits to same-sex partners has generally been "there is no money to do so." However, one could easily argue that economic restraints serve as a not-very-creative excuse to avoid a controversial issue, since there is no evidence that granting full partner benefits would increase costs. Indeed, one could argue that such a policy might save money since a likely consequence would be an increased presence of gay men and lesbians among the employees, and these persons are, perhaps, less likely than are heterosexual persons to require insurance for dependent children.

ATTITUDES TOWARD LESBIANS AND GAY MEN

Although institutional and governmental policies are an important target in eliminating homophobia, the assessment, understanding, and modification of individual attitudes are clearly relevant. (Indeed, policy and individual attitudes, being mutually interdependent, do not neatly separate.) Student organizations for lesbians and gay men exist at many undergraduate institutions in the United States, as do behaviors and incidents indicative of homophobia, such as verbal harassment and anti-gay violence. During the past two decades, the study of attitudes toward lesbians and gay men has been a growing area of research. One focus of this research has been the personality characteristics associated with negative beliefs about homosexuals (Kite, 1984). Investigators have also examined the various psychological functions which may be served by particular attitudes (Herek, 1986), as well as motivational factors involved in the expression of such attitudes (Herek, 1988). One of the more comprehensive studies was reported by Herek (1988). In a series of three studies of heterosexual students, he studied the association between homophobic attitudes—separated into attitudes toward gay men and attitudes toward lesbians—and attitudes toward women and traditional family ideology, as well as measures of dogmatism, ambiguity tolerance, conformity to peers, contact with gay men and lesbians, religiosity, psychological defensiveness, and insecure gender identity. Most of the scales studied were significantly associated with measures of homophobia in at least one of the three studies, and none was consistently and obviously a better predictor than others.

Jill Stevens, a colleague, and I conducted a study of attitudes toward gay men and lesbians designed to explore further the causes and correlates of homophobia. We gathered information from a group of undergraduates consisting of eighty-five women and sixty-six men. Of interest was the possibility of distinguishing between attitudes originating in an ideology (e.g., religion) versus attitudes expressed to emphasize one's gender identity (e.g., masculinity). To this end, we measured attitudes toward a variety of targets: gay men and lesbians (Daly, 1989), feminism and the women's movement (Fassinger, 1994), pornography (Stevens, DiLalla, and Le, 1995), animals, and vegetarianism. All scales had been psychometrically developed in previous research with the exception of scales measuring attitudes toward animals and toward vegetarianism, which were designed for this study. The attitudes toward animals scale assessed level of agreement with statements typical of animal rights activism (e.g., "snakes should not be killed when they're spotted on a hiking trail"). The attitudes toward vegetarianism scale emphasized stereotypes and included items such as "vegetarian men are not usually very masculine" and "vegetarians tend to have more energy than meat eaters." Thus, high scores on the animal scale are consistent with animal rights activism, whereas high scores on the vegetarian scale are consistent with negative attitudes toward vegetarians.

Research participants also completed other scales designed to assess individual traits and characteristics. Inherent in research on prejudice and discrimination is the fundamental issue of whether attitudes serve to enhance low self-esteem by implied contrast (Ehrlich, 1990). Thus, we expected that individuals' acceptance of themselves, as reflected in their self-esteem, would predict acceptance of lesbians and gay men. Accordingly, we employed the Self-Concept Scale (Stake, 1994) with subscales labeled Like, Task, Power, Vulnerability, Gifted, and Moral. Gender identity or sex role orientation was assessed with the Extended Personal Attributes Questionnaire (Spence and Helmreich, 1978) consisting of positive and negative masculinity and femininity scales.

Finally, we utilized the Social Paradigms Belief Inventory—a questionnaire designed by Kramer, Kahlbaugh, and Goldston (1992) to measure cognitive development. In their theoretical rationale, the authors divided cognitive development spanning adolescence through old age into three stages: absolute, relativistic, and dialectical. Absolute thinking is based in dichotomies and is mechanistic and reductionistic in outcome. Relativistic thinking is based on a world view that is contextual, unpredictable, and continually changing (Stevens, 1994). Some authors have suggested that this is a bridge rather than a stage since it precludes commitment and growth and, thus, motivates the individual to move on to the next stage. Dialectical thinking is the most mature style, allowing for confrontation and integration of contradictory ideas—a thinking style that renders one open to new ideas and facilitates the incorporation of new information and new concepts. We modified the scoring of the original scale somewhat in order to provide separate scores for each thinking style in addition to an overall score reflecting level of maturity. We predicted that less mature thinking would be associated with greater levels of homophobia, since those with absolute thinking styles tend to achieve understanding through dichotomization. Thus, they are likely to categorize attitudes into right-wrong, moral-immoral, heterosexual-homosexual. Although Kramer, Kahlbaugh, and Goldston (1992) initially viewed the development of thinking style as primarily age-related, their data suggest that persons mature at different rates and considerable variability may be found within a limited age range.[1]

Alpha coefficients for internal consistency were computed for all scales; all were over .70, indicating that, without exception, the scales achieved at least minimal requirements for reliability. The data were next analyzed according to sex. Compared to men, women were found to hold more positive attitudes toward animal rights, vegetarianism, and feminism and more negative attitudes toward pornography. On the self-concept scales, women scored higher than men on Moral (measuring loyalty/trustworthy/honest/law abiding) and on Like (measuring low self-confidence/easily hurt/self-conscious) than did men, while the remaining scales yielded small or no differences. These results are unremarkable and are consistent with sex role stereotypes. Only two of the four sex role orientation scales yielded significant sex differences: men scored higher than women on the negative masculine traits and lower than women on the positive feminine traits. These results are somewhat surprising: typically, women score significantly higher on both femininity scales and lower on both masculinity scales. The differences were in the expected direction but of small magnitude. Finally, only the absolute scale of the thinking style questionnaire yielded significant differences with women scoring lower than men. Men and women did not differ in their attitudes toward lesbians, but women were significantly more positive toward gay men than were men. Table 3.1 represents the mean values for men and women on the attitudes toward lesbians and gay men scales.

Of primary interest were the associations between attitudes toward gay men and lesbians and scores on the other scales. Correlation coefficient matrices were computed. Since there were statistically significant sex differences on many of the scales, these analyses were conducted separately for women and men. Thus, there were four sets of correlations distinguished by the sex of the research participant and the sex of the attitude target (lesbians, gay men). The significant correlation coefficients are presented in Table 3.2. The reader may note that there were conspicuously more significant correlations for women than for men—particularly when the target was lesbians. Furthermore, for women, but not for men, the sources of association were identical for lesbians and gay men, although the magnitude of the associations varied. For women, positive attitudes toward lesbians and gay men were associated with positive attitudes towards animals and vegetarians, a self-concept highlighted by feelings of being powerful/strong/dominant and creative/having innate talent, and low measures of absolute or dichotomous thinking. For men, there were no significant associations between attitudes toward lesbians and any other scale; more positive attitudes toward gay men were associated with positive attitudes toward vegetarians and feminism and with low levels of absolute thinking.

The patterns of correlations were internally consistent and logically coherent. The correlation between attitudes toward gay men and attitudes toward lesbians was .913 for women and .676 for men. These suggest an extremely high association, particularly for women, whose data indicate almost identical attitudes. Furthermore, the patterns tended to reflect conformity with liberal political beliefs. Indeed, we also asked participants to indicate their political preference along a continuum varying from very conservative to very liberal; correlations between political preference and attitudes to-

TABLE 3.1. Attitudes Toward Gay Men*—Means for Women and Men

	Attitudes Toward Lesbians	Attitudes Toward Gay Men
Women	3.26	3.64
Men	3.40	2.99

* From a scale of 1 = Strongly Disagree to 5 = Strongly Agree

TABLE 3.2. Attitudes Toward Gay Men and Lesbians—Significant Correlations with Other Scales for Men and Women

	Attitudes Toward Lesbians	Attitudes Toward Gay Men
Women:		
Animals	.340	.363
Vegetarians	−.319	−.393
Absolute	−.281	−.275
Power	.281	.246
Gifted	.263	.228
Men:		
Vegetarians		−.364
Absolute		−.246
Feminism		.266

ward gay men and lesbians were significantly correlated for both men and women, although the implied associations were not particularly strong (correlation coefficients ranging from .22 to .42).

Discussion

Perhaps the most interesting results were the significant correlations for both men and women indicating an association between a proclivity toward absolute thinking and negative attitudes toward gay men and lesbians. Thus, persons who structure their world in terms of simple dichotomies (right and wrong, black and white, good and bad, heterosexual and homosexual) have a readily available scapegoat with which to gain psychological solace and maintain self-esteem in the face of failure. Furthermore, these data suggest a common denominator for various prejudicial attitudes—persons who rely on absolute thinking may readily resort to an "us-them" cognitive structure in times of conflict and threat. According to theories of moral exclusion, an "us-them" worldview allows individuals to participate in discriminatory and prejudicial behaviors with little guilt. "Moral exclusion," defined by Opotow (1990a) is: ". . . when individuals or groups are perceived as *outside the boundary in which moral values, rules, and considerations of fairness apply.* Those who are morally excluded are perceived as nonentities, expendable, or undeserving; consequently, harming them appears acceptable, appropriate, or just" (p. 1, emphasis in the original). Immature or absolute thinking predisposes the individual to perceive people as good (their group) or bad (other groups) (Deutsch, 1990) and to view heterosexuality and homosexuality as salient dichotomous traits (Kramer, Kahlbaugh, and Goldston, 1992). In contrast, nonabsolute pluralistic or dialectical thinking ". . . fosters creative problem solving, openness, lack of defensiveness, flexibility . . ." (Opotow, 1990b, p. 177).

In the present study, there was a consistent tendency for men to express more hostile attitudes than women, especially toward gay men. These data are consistent with previous research (Engstrom, 1997; Logan, 1996; Whitley and Kite, 1995). Herek (1988) proposed an interpretation of these sex differences in the context of the patterns of correlations he noted between homophobia and other attitudes: women's negative attitudes toward gay men and lesbians originate in ideological concerns (religious beliefs, family values, and gender ideology); men's prejudicial attitudes share similar sources but, in addition, are a response to a need to defend their gender identity: ". . . the male sex role in contemporary America explicitly emphasizes the importance of heterosexuality to masculinity, and many males also feel the need to affirm their masculinity by rejecting men who violate the heterosexual norm" (p. 472). The results of this study are somewhat supportive of Herek's interpretations. Women's attitudes toward lesbians varied linearly and predictably with their attitudes toward gay men, and the correlates were the same for both attitude measures. In contrast, men's attitudes toward gay men and lesbians were significantly correlated, but to a lesser extent, and did not exhibit similar relationships with other scales. Thus, Herek's proposal is supported by the similarity in target attitudes found for women and the dissimilarity found for men, as well as by the finding that attitudes toward gay men and lesbians seemed to be consistent with an identifiable worldview for women while target attitudes were somewhat more isolated from other attitudes for men. Yet, this hypothesis also predicts that men's, rather than women's, homophobic attitudes are associated with sex role orientation and self-concept; in the present study, women, and not men, were found to exhibit this pattern. This implies that men's attitudes, although isolated from an overall worldview, were not apparently predicted by high or low levels of masculinity nor by positive or negative self-concept. The data did indicate that women who believed themselves to be strong, competent, powerful, talented, and creative had somewhat positive attitudes toward lesbians and gay men.

CRITIQUE

Legislative bodies, university administrators, and corporate management often express frustration when attempting to address activists' demands—the demands multiply and the issues change. Surely, governmental bodies who magnanimously gave women the vote assumed they would finally go home and forever be too busy cooking to vote. From the activists' perspective, these reconstructions are not only to be expected but are necessary as theory, action, and outcome are mutually interdependent. Kramer's theory of cognitive development predicts that, "A synthesis . . . [occurs] . . . which allows for the growth of one's knowledge by integration of new information. . . . Dialectical thinking is a continuous, creative process whereby new beliefs are born out of the synthesis of contradictory knowledge" (Stevens, 1994, p. 3). As individuals mature, so do political movements.

Feminism is frequently taken as a model (albeit a rough and imperfect one) for the struggle for gay and lesbian rights (Warner,

1993). Since the early 1970s, feminism has traversed many definitions, manifestations, meanings, and goals. Initially, the goal of feminism was equality with men in employment and education. An essential similarity between the two movements is the discovery—the overwhelming and surprising awareness—of the manner in which society is structured. This is recognized as the primacy of the male gender in the case of feminism and the primacy of heterosexuality in the case of gay rights: ". . . queer theory is opening up in the way that feminism did when feminists began treating gender more and more as a primary category for understanding problems that did not initially look gender-specific" (Warner, 1993, p. xiv). Just as feminists have, over several decades, documented the incredible pervasiveness of gender as an organizing principle in human relations, politics, economics, education, employment, and justice, so those working against homophobia have recognized the ubiquitous domination and influence of heterosexuality:

> Every person who comes to a queer self-understanding knows in one way or another that her stigmatization is connected with gender, the family, notions of individual freedom, the state, public speech, consumption and desire, nature and culture, maturation, reproductive politics, racial and national fantasy, class identity, truth and trust, censorship, intimate life and social display, terror and violence, health care, and deep cultural norms about the bearing of the body. (Warner, 1993, p. xiii)

The increasingly deep and elaborate levels of awareness regarding heterosexism necessitate the transformation of goals beyond mere "equality" to more complex, reciprocating, and multilayered issues.

As feminists evolved from penitents to critics, scholars, and purveyors of culture, theory progressed. Feminists came to the realization that they did not wish to win but to change the rules. In other words, they wished not only for equality, but for an entirely different culture. Many feminists found success climbing the corporate ladder surprisingly unfulfilling. They began to define success in their own terms rather than according to patriarchal values. They prefer a society in which nurturance and friendship are valued over dominance, in which protection rather than exploitation of the environment is the ideal, and in which laws, institutions, and corporations are designed for psychological and physical well-being rather than for the accumulation of power and wealth. They have begun to bring to traditional male arenas their own uniqueness rather than adopting the values of men.

Gay and lesbian activists have struggled with similar issues. The initial goal was equality and, in order to achieve this, efforts were aimed at being found "acceptable," and demonstrating a lack of threat—essentially to provide convincing evidence that homosexuality and heterosexuality were not "really" different from one another. The criteria for claiming partner benefits described previously are those which basically describe a traditional heterosexual spouse, that is, the legal joining of money and property. The message conveyed by such criteria is "we will give you partner benefits if you act like us, love like us, live like us." As with giving women the vote, management hoped that by providing partner benefits, gay men and lesbian employees would, once again, become invisible—take their health care and go home to their domestic partners. However, as the theoretical underpinnings of the activist movement develop and mature, awareness and insight expand and the goals are reconstructed. As with feminists, many gay and lesbian activists now wish to "change the rules." They no longer wish to participate as equals in existing structures, but to share in the construction of new and better ones.

Warner (1993) defines the reconstruction: "Because the logic of the sexual order is so deeply embedded by now in an indescribably wide range of social institutions, and is embedded in the most standard accounts of the world, queer struggles aim not just at toleration or equal status but at challenging those institutions and accounts" (p. xiii). In a similar vein, Tierney (1997) advises scholars: "The purpose of queer studies is more than simply the production of queer theory. Queer theorists advocate change and become involved in the change processes" (p. 62). Throughout his book, Tierney employs the metaphor of being invited to dinner—invited to sit at the table. The goal is no longer to be included in the academic canon as one more minority group but rather ". . . to empower lesbian, gay and bisexual people to attain the forces of production so that they are, in effect, not invited to the table, but participate mutually in the construction of the table" (p. 64). Minority races, women, gay men, and lesbians have found a limited measure of acceptance and equality if they "behave." If women wear power suits and work at their jobs eighteen hours a day, they can be "successful" and they can be "equal." If gay men and lesbians do not prominently display photos of their partners, if they do not dress in drag for Gay Pride Day, if they do not reveal who they are to their military cohorts, they, too, can be invited to dinner. But this is hardly what it has been labeled—"appreciation of diversity." Where is the diversity?

"Queer theory . . . contributes to the self-clarification of the struggles and wishes of the age, it may make the world queerer than ever" (Warner, 1993, p. xxviii). And what exactly is a "world queerer than ever?" We won't know until we are there but we can predict that, in order to get there, gay men and lesbians must not be merely "acceptable," but rather appreciated, admired, and respected. In discussing the negative effects of homophobia, Hogan and Rentz (1996) comment: ". . . healthy gay male and lesbian identity development requires positive interactions with heterosexual individuals" (p. 309). I agree, but emphatically add that healthy heterosexual identity development requires positive interactions with lesbians and gay men.

The study of attitudes described above is an example of the "acceptance" model. When initiating this research project, we attempted to locate questionnaires to assess the constructs of interest. When evaluating questionnaires designed to evaluate attitudes toward gay men and lesbians, our primary concerns were to use instruments that had separate scales for gay men and lesbians and that had good psychometric properties (e.g., reliability and validity). We believed we had found a good questionnaire to measure the constructs of interest. Yet, only two years later, the choice seems outdated.

The questionnaires we were able to locate that were designed to assess attitudes toward homosexuality (including the one used in this study) can be criticized on the basis of content which, in hindsight, seems to collude with heterosexual privilege. Table 3.1 represents the actual mean values for men and women on the scales measuring attitudes toward lesbians and gay men. The scoring for the scale was 1 ("strongly disagree") to 5 ("strongly agree") with 3 reflecting "no opinion." High scores reflect "positive attitudes." In the study reported above, all means were around 3.00 and most between 3.00 and 4.00. The common interpretation of these data has been and is that undergraduates do not hold negative views about homosexuality but appear to be either mildly positive or indifferent. At first glance, this seems to be inconsistent with the claims of harassment and violence against gay men and lesbians commonly reported on campuses and in the community.

However, a far more discouraging interpretation of these data emerges if one examines the content of the items. Examples include: "I would not feel uncomfortable being around a man I knew was gay," "I don't think female homosexuality is morally wrong," and "I don't think there are some jobs that lesbians should be prohibited from having." In fact, the content of these scales reflects the presence or absence of negative attitudes rather than the presence or absence of positive attitudes. Scoring in the "no-opinion" range for the item: "It wouldn't bother me to be neighbors with a woman I knew was a lesbian" implies that the individual is uncertain—having a lesbian neighbor may, indeed, be a problem. Contrast this with a "no-opinion" score for the item "My life would be enriched if I had lesbian friends." Here a "3" implies the possibility of benefits rather than the possibility of no harm. In other words, the questionnaires designed to measure attitudes toward gay men and lesbians reinforce the idea that the best that can be hoped for is "acceptance"—to not be fired, to not be hated, to not be the target of violence. The possibility of being hired or admired as a lesbian or gay man is not considered.

As the goals of activism are reconstructed, the solutions and strategies must be reconstructed as well. Again, the developmental cognitive model of Kramer, Kahlbaugh, and Goldston (1992) might be adapted in order to understand the political development of gay and lesbian activism. The more recent theories and actions embrace the notion of dialectics. At the most elemental level, dialectical strategies are ones that are not stable, internally consistent, or universal but are instead flexible, potentially contradictory, and situation-specific. The very definition of dialectics assumes continual adaptation and, therefore, change. In such a context, we expect goals, solutions, and strategies to change, grow, and transform; indeed, we should question their effectiveness if they remain static. Theories of sexual orientation in the 1990s have focused on two opposing models: essentialism (genetic, biological, and/or hormonal "causes" of homosexuality) and social constructionism (the construction of homosexuality, as well as heterosexuality, by social, political, and cultural forces). The essentialist position has gained popularity in recent years with claims by medical and psychological researchers to have discovered the neurological basis of sexual orientation. Some gay men and lesbians embraced this new research with the hope that this new spin on homosexuality would elicit less homophobia—perhaps homosexuals should be pitied rather than hated; they cannot help their sexual orientation; certainly, they cannot be blamed. However, consistent with a dialectical understanding of continuity, homophobia was, in turn, reconstructed. The "new spin" became a transformation from "psychologically sick and evil" to "genetically deformed" with the developing possibility of genetic engineers weeding out what they believe to be the homosexual genes as they perfect the ideal fetus. What appears to offer a positive direction for those wishing for liberation and enlightenment becomes, when interpreted in a different context, yet one more route to oppression.

Within a dialectical framework, Kitzinger (1995) examined the contradictions both between and within essentialism and social constructionism. Kitzinger's sympathies clearly lie with the social constructionists: ". . . arguing that we were born that way . . . is intended to suggest that homosexuality is 'natural' . . . the assumption being that what is natural is both ethically acceptable and politically unchangeable. Feminists have spent more than a century challenging concepts of the natural which relegate women to the kitchen and the bedroom and justify and condone male subjugation of women" (p. 153). Furthermore, she notes that the collection of empirical evidence cannot, due the very nature of the question, resolve the issue. Nevertheless, she concludes that ". . . the apparent outcome of the debate, the persistence and continuing parallel development of *both* logically incompatible theoretical frameworks, is advantageous for the growth and vitality of both lesbian and gay psychology and the lesbian and gay movements" (Kitzinger, 1995,

p. 150, emphasis in the original). Some would label Kitzinger's work as contradictory and logically indefensible—I would label it dialectical and progressive.

Although acceptance is certainly an improvement over oppression and violence, a dialectical transformation of gay and lesbian activism must occur in order to ". . . go beyond calling for tolerance of lesbians and gays. [And to] . . . assert the necessarily and desirably queer nature of the world" (Warner, 1993, p. xxi). A crucial and necessary component of this process is the recognition that there is no single answer, no one process that will provide a complete, unambiguous, and conceptually consistent solution yielding universal respect and justice. Since persons who oppress others continue to create new structures, new laws, and new systems of logic to justify and rationalize discrimination and oppression, so must those who wish to gain respect, appreciation, and justice.

NOTE

1. Further boring methodological details are available from the author upon request.

REFERENCES

Bohan, J. S. (1996). *Psychology and sexual orientation*. New York: Routledge.
Daly, J. (1989). *Measuring attitudes toward lesbians and gay men: Development and initial psychometric evaluation of an instrument.* Unpublished Dissertation. Southern Illinois University, Carbondale, Illinois.
Deutsch, M. (1990). Psychological roots of moral exclusion. *Journal of Social Issues, 46*(1), 21-25.
Ehrlich, H. J. (1990). The ecology of anti-gay violence. *Journal of Interpersonal Violence, 5*(3), 359-365.
Engstrom, C. M. (1997). Attitudes of heterosexual students toward their gay male and lesbian peers. *Journal of College Student Development, 38*(6), 565-576.
Fassinger, R. E. (1994). Development and testing of the attitudes toward feminism and the women's movement (FWM) scale. *Psychology of Women Quarterly, 18*(4), 389-402.
Herek, G. M. (1986). On heterosexual masculinity. *American Behavioral Scientist, 29*(5), 563-577.
Herek, G. M. (1988). Heterosexuals' attitudes toward lesbians and gay men: Correlates and gender differences. *Journal of Sex Research, 25*(4), 451-477.

Hogan, T. L. and Rentz, A. L. (1996). Homophobia in the academy. *Journal of College Student Development, 37*(3), 309-314.

Human Rights Campaign Quarterly. (1997). Report from the job front. Spring, 12-13.

Kite, M. E. (1984). Sex differences in attitudes toward homosexuals: A meta-analytic review. *Journal of Homosexuality, 10*(1/2), 69-81.

Kitzinger, C. (1995). Social constructionism: Implications for lesbian and gay psychology. In R. D'Augelli and C. J. Patterson (Eds.), *Lesbian, gay, and bisexual identities over the lifespan: Psychological perspectives.* New York: Oxford University Press.

Kramer, D. A., Kahlbaugh, P. E., and Goldston, R. B. (1992). A measure of paradigm beliefs about the social world. *Journal of Gerontology, 47*(3), 180-189.

Logan, C. R. (1996). Homophobia? No, homoprejudice. *Journal of Homosexuality, 31*(3), 31-53.

Opotow, S. (1990a). Moral exclusion and injustice: An introduction. *Journal of Social Issues, 46*(1), 1-20.

Opotow, S. (1990b). Deterring moral exclusion. *Journal of Social Issues, 46*(1), 173-182.

Spence, J. T. and Helmreich, R. L. (1978). *Masculinity and femininity: Their psychological dimensions, correlates, and antecedents.* Austin, TX: University of Texas Press.

Stake, J. E. (1994). Development and validation of the six-factor self-concept scale for adults. *Educational and Psychological Measurement, 54*(1), 56-72.

Stevens, J. (1994). *Relationship between personality traits and level of cognitive structural organization.* Unpublished Master's Thesis, Southern Illinois University, Carbondale, Illinois.

Stevens, J., DiLalla, D., and Le, M. (1995). *Pornography and sexualized violence: Links between attitudes and exposure.* Paper presented at Midwestern Psychological Association, Chicago.

Tierney, W. G. (1997). *Academic outlaws.* Thousand Oaks, CA: Sage.

Warner, M. (1993). Introduction. In M. Warner (Ed.), *Fear of a queer planet: Queer politics and social theory.* Minneapolis: University of Minnesota Press.

Whitley, B. E. and Kite, M. E. (1995). Sex differences in attitudes toward homosexuality: A comment on Oliver and Hyde (1993). *Psychological Bulletin, 117*(1), 146-154.

Zuckerman, A. J. and Simons, G. F. (1994). *Sexual orientation in the workplace.* Santa Cruz, CA: International Partners Press.

Chapter 4

Internalized Homophobia and Therapeutic Efficacy

Elizabeth Johnson

Oppression of lesbians and gay men is currently widespread and includes overt hate expressed through acts and attitudes of hostility, exclusion, and discrimination, as well as through attitudes of ignorance and omission. This system of negativity toward homosexuals is regularly called homophobia, although researchers and clinicians have challenged the accuracy and usefulness of this term. Sophie (1987), for example, states that the term *homophobia* is often used as an analogy to irrational fear, which suggests that the hate and discrimination is a mental disorder. Kitzinger (1996) prefers the term *heterosexism*—a word which is modeled on political concepts rather than a disorder of some kind.

An important conceptual advance in clinical psychodynamic theory was made by Malyon (1982), who discussed the impact of heterosexist, homophobic surroundings on psychological development in homosexuals. Malyon observed that the biased environment and socialization results in what he referred to as "internalized homophobia." He did not view homosexuality as pathological per se; instead, he saw pathology as sometimes resulting from the harmful effects of oppressive socialization.

Shidlo (1994) wrote that when gay people blame themselves, rather than a homophobic society, for the problems they experience as gay people, it is internalized homophobia. Perkins (1996) criti-

The author wishes to thank Jan Talbot for her comments on an earlier draft of this chapter.

cized the use of the term *internalized homophobia* on the grounds that it reformulates oppression as a psychological problem at the individual level. Shidlo (1994) suggested using "internalized homo-negativism" as an alternative because it is more sensitive to the cultural/social context. However, following Malyon's (1982) intro-duction of the concept, *internalized homophobia* has been the most common term used in the literature to designate hate turned inward.

Purcell and Hicks (1996) postulated that internalized homopho-bia and general homophobia are perpetuated by the official sanc-tioning of discrimination by the institutions of courts, legislatures, and the military. Internalized homophobia has been shown to be exacerbated or to resurface after a hate attack (Herek, 1996). Family levels of homophobia may affect levels of internalized homophobia (Nungesser, 1983), as do personal variables such as each individu-al's strengths and vulnerabilities.

Clinicians and researchers have identified thoughts, feelings, and behaviors that seem to indicate internalized homophobia. Falco (1996) described one manifestation of internalized homophobia in lesbians as a searching for the "reason" they are gay, as if lesbian-ism is a deviation from normal. Falco noted other indications such as uneasiness with the idea of children being raised by lesbians, being attracted to unavailable women only, having a high level of distrust of others, or experiencing somatic symptoms related to feelings about one's lesbianism. Other signs of internalized homo-phobia have included a tolerance of discriminatory or abusive treat-ment from others or a tendency to sabotage career goals (Gonsio-rek, 1988). Malyon (1982) conceptualized internalized homophobia as both conscious and unconscious, which would then make the symptoms of self-hate more complex.

Ross and Rosser (1996) have pointed out the need for better construct validity in studies of internalized homophobia. Shidlo (1994) suggested that a precision instrument for measuring internal-ized homophobia would be useful for identifying gay people with either small or large amounts of the construct. Ross and Rosser developed an empirical scale designed to measure the construct of internalized homophobia in men who have sex with men. Four dimensions of internalized homophobia were identified: (1) con-cern about public identification as gay; (2) perceptions of stigma associated with being gay, both within the gay community and outside; (3) social comfort with gay men; and (4) concern about the moral and religious acceptability of being gay. The scale was shown to demonstrate concurrent validity when compared to criterion measures. The four dimensions identified were associated with variables that had been identified as clinically related to internalized homophobia.

Researchers have suggested that practically all lesbian and gay persons internalize homophobia to some extent (Cabaj, 1996a). Shidlo (1994) indicated a need for research on issues such as whether levels of internalized homophobia are consistent throughout adulthood. Prevalence studies have found higher levels of internalized homophobia in gay men who had been sexually abused as children (Knisely, 1992). Jones and Hill (1996) found internalized homophobia in African Americans to be particularly troubling due to the resultant inhibited ability to combat what is usually a hostile, homophobic, and racist environment.

Despite widespread persecution and its internalization, researchers have found base rates of psychological disturbance to be roughly parallel in homosexual and heterosexual populations (Gonsiorek, 1982). Although rates of depression or suicide are not elevated in gays and lesbians, of those who do consult mental health professionals, signs of internalized homophobia such as depression are very common (Downey and Friedman, 1996). Some have suggested that, due to the different stressors on lesbian women versus non-lesbian women, mitigating factors for depression may differ even though overall rates of the mood disorder are the same.

Researchers have attempted to measure psychological distress caused by internalized homophobia in lesbians and gay men, and have studied both levels and types of distress (Wagner, Brondolo, and Rabkin, 1996; Shidlo, 1994). Malyon (1982) suggested that internalized homophobia causes depression and influences identity formation, self-esteem, the elaboration of defenses, patterns of cognition, psychological integrity, object relations, and superego functioning. He saw the effects as resulting in a suppression of gay feelings, usually in a temporary manner, but still interrupting the process of identity growth.

Shidlo (1994) found a high level of internalized homophobia to be significantly associated with overall psychological distress and other specific measures of adjustment, including lowered self-esteem, greater loneliness, lower social support, and less satisfaction with that support. Nungesser (1983) developed the Nungesser Homosexual Attitudes Inventory, which assesses internalized homophobia with a twenty-item scale.

Wagner, Brondolo, and Rabkin (1996) used the Nungesser inventory to study internalized homophobia in HIV-positive men and the relationship to distress and coping. The researchers found positive correlations between internalized homophobia and all self-report measures of psychological distress at both baseline and follow-up two years later. Other researchers have found direct correlations between internalized homophobia and the tendency to devalue other gays, to limit one's career achievements, to fail in intimate relationships, to suffer anxiety or depression, and to act out in self-destructive behaviors (Stein and Cabaj, 1996).

Relationships between internalized homophobia and other symptoms and behaviors have also been reported. Stein (1996) proposed that the levels of internalized homophobia in the members of lesbian and gay families influence the members' ability to respond to the stresses of societal oppression. Klinger (1996) proposed that unexamined homophobia can be a negative factor in lesbian couple relationships if it leads to one or both partners lacking confidence in the viability of the relationship. Klinger and Stein (1996) suggested that internalized homophobia may complicate adult adjustment to childhood sexual abuse.

Cabaj (1996c) observed a connection between societal homophobia and internalized homophobia and the reinforced use of alcohol and other drugs. The report found that many gays and lesbians had their first same-sex sexual experience while drinking or intoxicated in order to overcome internal fear, denial, anxiety, or even revulsion about gay sex. Cabaj pointed out that substance abuse may then become linked to sexual expression and persist to the point of becoming part of one's identity.

Malyon (1982) proposed that homonegative attitudes are incorporated into the person's self-image and cause a fragmentation of sexual and emotional facets that interferes with the developmental process. Wagner, Brondolo, and Rabkin (1996) conceptualized internalized homophobia as consisting of low self-acceptance and high self-loathing; these are connected to low self-esteem and then serve as the link to psychological distress.

Shidlo (1994) proposed that some of what has been termed unconscious homophobia may, instead, be the diffuse intrapsychic consequences of conscious internalized homophobia. A similar conceptualization has been put forth by Falco (1996); she stated that lesbians' non-disclosure for reasons of safety could lead to a self-censoring rigidity that may generalize to interpersonal relationships. According to Falco (1996), "when the self is thus constricted, self-esteem often deteriorates, for the psyche tends to interpret *hidden aspects* of the self as *bad* aspects" (p. 401, emphasis in the original).

A variety of theories and research on overcoming the effects of internalized homophobia exist. Ross (1996) found that the social structure and support that comes with acculturation into the gay subculture is important with respect to the sexual safety habits of gay men. Those who were better acculturated engaged in less risky sex. Seibt et al. (1995) suggested that, among gay men, acculturation and overall health are associated, just as acculturation and health have been shown to be associated in migrant communities.

Sophie (1987) has identified six effective coping strategies used by lesbians coming out: cognitively restructuring the meanings of internalized homophobia; avoiding premature self-labeling with a negative identity; adopting temporary self-labels for the sake of exploration; engaging in self-disclosure; meeting others who are lesbian; and habituating to lesbianism. Cognitively restructuring the meanings of internalized homophobia occurs in much the same way that one would alter irrational ideas. Adopting a negative identity by, for example, refraining from labeling oneself until one can view the sexual identity in a neutral or positive way needs to be avoided. Temporarily calling oneself bisexual or quickly identifying oneself as lesbian may help in finding others to identify with. Self-disclosure may be important for intimacy, confirmation of identity, and self-actualization. Meeting and socializing with other lesbians can help facilitate cognitive restructuring, provide role models, and lead to lesbianism being understood as ordinary rather than unusual.

PSYCHOTHERAPY AND INTERNALIZED HOMOPHOBIA

Researchers have criticized the use of psychotherapy for overcoming internalized homophobia. Perkins (1996) and Kitzinger (1996) both stated that therapy, even if attempting to emphasize the effects of outside oppression, should not be the answer because it seeks solutions in the mind rather than in biased social and political structures. Perkins (1996) sees psychotherapy as harmful to the lesbian community in the sense that it "privatizes pain" and focuses on deficits rather than strengths (p. 77). She hypothesizes that the popularity of therapy with lesbians is probably also a reflection of perceived deficits in lesbian communities. In that light, one's use of psychotherapy could be seen as a manifestation of internalized homophobia.

When working with gay men and lesbians in psychotherapy, Gonsiorek (1982) recommends differentiating sexual identity crises from psychiatric pathology. The author details how both Axis I and Axis II diagnostic categories may, at times, seem to overlap with the symptoms of sexual identity crisis, internalized homophobia, and/or symptoms specific to related environmental stressors. An example used involves the appearance of characterological-looking ego differentiation and boundary confusion that might be seen in a person going through a huge sexual-identity struggle.

Stein and Cabaj (1996) stress that the therapist's explicit acceptance and acknowledgment of the client's homosexuality is a central factor in therapy with gay men. The client is helped to accept himself by experiencing acceptance from others, including the therapist. The therapy relationship itself is a treatment modality, for better or for worse (Sophie, 1987). The therapist is seen as a representative of society and needs to convey acceptance of homosexuality without minimizing the real obstacles.

A critical asset for therapists working with gay and lesbian clients appears to be an awareness of the process of internalized homophobia and of the cultural milieu of heterosexism. It has been suggested that gay therapists might be better able to understand these issues (Cabaj, 1996b). Malyon (1982) recommended what he called "gay-affirmative" psychotherapy, which pinpoints homophobia and its internalization as a major pathological variable in the development of some symptomatic conditions among gay men (p. 62). Malyon's gay-affirmative approach has emphasized the importance of providing corrective experiences in order to ameliorate the consequences of biased socialization. Malyon's conception of such psychotherapy is psychodynamically-based and focuses on conflict resolution and self-actualization. Four stages are delineated:

1. The stage of "therapeutic alliance" is built largely by the therapist's expression of positive values toward homosexuality.
2. The "analytic phase" involves resolving conflict and cognitive restructuring (i.e., seeking out the effects of internalized homophobia in developmental arrest and decreased self-concept).
3. The "identity consolidation phase" includes the consolidation of a gay identity, as a "second-epoch adolescence," and the facilitation of capacity for intimacy.
4. The "existential phase" involves finding gay-affirmative meaning and purpose in individualized solutions.

Ross and Rosser (1996) argue that the first stage of therapy with gays is to identify the presence and nature of internalized homophobia. Others maintain that the reduction of internalized homophobia can be considered an important measure of the success of both therapies and prevention efforts (Malyon, 1982; Sophie, 1987). Falco (1996) found that women with decreased internalized homophobia can reach "a true integration and a working through of the losses and choices involved in loving another woman" (p. 399).

Sophie (1987) theorized that because internalized homophobia makes a lesbian identity very threatening to a woman's self-esteem, there is a need to reduce internalized homophobia for the individual to accept a lesbian identity without compromised self-esteem. Sophie suggests evaluating clients' achievement of a positive sexual identity by assessing improvement in internalized homophobia. Signs of improvement would include (a) comfort with and respect and admiration for other lesbians and gays; (b) comfort with one's own feelings about relations with women and fantasies about women; (c) the ability to form a meaningful relationship with another woman; (d) positive self-disclosures to others; and (e) the use of a homopositive reference group.

Downey and Friedman (1996) offer a number of caveats concerning psychotherapy and internalized homophobia. They differentiate between what they call "primary" and "secondary" internalized homophobia. Those with primary internalized homophobia are defined as those lacking significant Axis I or Axis II psychopathology, who come to the therapy with internalized homophobia as their major source of distress. Those with secondary internalized homophobia are those with histories of serious abuse, neglect, or psychic trauma; these are individuals who have experienced self-hate long before they are exposed to social input about homosexuality.

Gay or lesbian persons with early trauma may experience the older issues disguised and condensed in the conscious perception of conflicted feelings about being gay (Downey and Friedman, 1996). Traumatized gays and lesbians are more likely to experience all relationships, including the therapeutic relationship, as problematic. The authors express the importance of matching the appropriate type of therapy (e.g., supportive versus insight) to client type.

Downey and Friedman (1996) define supportive therapy as largely psychoeducational, structured, and focused on problem-solving, confrontation, and challenge, whether gay-affirmative or not. Insight therapy is defined as that which affords more emphasis on uncovering and exploration, and allows room for mixed feelings. The authors found that clients with primary internalized homophobia, where the ability to love and to work has been preserved, did well with supportive therapy. However, the lesbian or gay clients with secondary internalized homophobia were likely to respond much better to insight psychotherapy, and stood a moderate-to-high chance of actually getting worse if/when treated with supportive therapy.

A MODEL FOR INCREASED THERAPEUTIC EFFICACY

Researchers have shown the importance of decreasing internalized homophobia in clients who are suffering its effects. Other writers have emphasized aspects of psychotherapy such as the need for acceptance by the therapist and for informed cautious exploration of client attitudes and issues that seem to be critical in making such improvement. In the remainder of this chapter, I propose a model for increasing therapeutic efficacy when internalized homophobia is significant.

The model draws upon current research and is informed by my findings in working with clients, as well as in supervising and consulting with other psychotherapists. My own therapeutic approach is an integrated one and is grounded in psychodynamic understanding, self-psychology, and feminist theory. The broad goals implicit in such a model are to decrease internalized homophobia and psychological distress, and to increase emotional and cognitive growth, self-esteem, and overall psychological functioning. However, there are three particular sub-goals of the therapeutic process which should be emphasized for clients struggling with internalized homophobia; these are more specific requisite parts of the broader general goals and present unique therapy challenges. The sub-goals are (a) to address the impact of internalized homophobia on the establishment of a working therapy alliance; (b) to increase awareness of internalized homophobic attitudes in the context of the client's level of functioning and the anticipated treatment goals; and (c) to increase insight into connections between internalized homophobia and factors such as external stressors, personal history, and self-esteem. In the following sections, I will discuss these goals and the challenges associated with achieving them, as well as present suggestions for implementation. Two case studies will be described to illustrate applied examples.

The Establishment of a Working Therapy Alliance

Clients with significant internalized homophobia may have more difficulty establishing a therapeutic relationship than other gay and lesbian clients. One reason for this may have to do with the likelihood that clients with high internalized homophobia will also be the clients with a history of trauma, although that doesn't mean that every client with internalized homophobia comes with a history of other abuse or neglect. For adequate trust to develop and a working relationship to form, it is important that the therapist finds the appropriate balance between assuming enough beneficial power to effect change, but not so much as to be a negative factor. Wielding too much power can oppress and victimize the client. Also, oppressed individuals are often sensitive to a power imbalance in relationships with authority figures, so the therapist can help establish a working alliance by being alert about how he or she is perceived.

As with other early work in psychotherapy, it is crucial to assess the primary interpersonal dynamics that inhibit intimacy and relationship formation. Such dynamics can be specific to the individual's personality and style, or derived from the surroundings. The therapist must be sensitive to environmental and internalized influences specific to homosexuality to accurately assess certain interpersonal impasses.

Clients with a high level of internalized homophobia may be less aware of issues of interpersonal safety if they have a high tendency toward self-blame and self-deprecation. For example, instead of fear, the client may express feeling "paranoid" about the therapy. Along similar lines, the subtypes of internalized homophobia referred to earlier (e.g., Ross, 1996) and the degree of each subtype present in each client may lead to impasses in the development of a therapeutic relationship that are specific to each subtype.

For most gay clients, a therapist perceived as unfriendly toward gays is not likely to be trusted enough to work with. However, clients with high levels of concern about being publicly identified as gay may prefer a therapist who does not specialize in work with gay men or lesbians, so as to better hide in the therapy setting. This may also be true for clients attempting to deny their sexual orientation to themselves. Clients who perceive a great deal of social stigma attached to being gay might also have mixed feelings, consciously and unconsciously, about working with a gay-friendly therapist.

Other aspects of the same conundrum are likely to arise when clients make assumptions about the therapist's sexual orientation, even though the therapist's sexual orientation will be more critical to some lesbian and gay clients than others. Therapists perceived as gay are more likely assumed to be gay-friendly, but are not always preferred initially as the therapist of choice. Gay clients who agree with some moral/religious judgments made against lesbians and gay men, for example, may be unable to work with a therapist whom they perceive will not accept their mixed and/or negative beliefs about homosexuality.

Clients with a high level of discomfort around other gays (including themselves) may prefer a therapist they perceive as straight, insofar as they wish for a degree of identification with the therapist. Clients with high levels of public identification concerns and high levels of perceived social stigma may fear that a homosexual therapist will expect them to adopt a more public persona, to socialize more with gays and lesbians, or to express only positive feelings about being gay.

The clients with high internalized homophobia may devalue the therapist in the way that they assign stigma to themselves. They may be unaware or unable to articulate these assumptions, although such assumptions can interfere with forming the working alliance. Thus, the therapist's assessment of the above issues is critical in terms of reaching the therapy goal.

Therefore, the most important considerations in forming a treatment relationship are to assess concurrently the client's perceptions of therapist attitudes about homosexuality and the threats to intimacy which are unique to the individual's personality organization and overlaid by the influence of homophobic socialization. Both the importance and the difficulty of achieving these goals may be greater when persons have higher levels of internalized homophobia.

The stronger the client's discomfort in the first part of therapy, the more critical it is for the therapist to initiate, in a timely manner, discussion of such an observation. The therapist can encourage a nonjudgmental exploration by the use of comments such as "I wonder what it is about my silence (being here, etc.) that bothers you the most." These issues must be at least partly verbalized as a prerequisite for an adequately secure therapy alliance. A partial working through may be required quickly to prevent premature, even immediate, termination. An unfortunate consequence of premature termination is the possibility that the relationship failure will reinforce preexisting beliefs about the inferior gay self and/or external oppression.

Increasing Awareness of Internalized Homophobic Attitudes

The second goal for clients with internalized homophobia is to increase awareness of the internalized homophobic attitudes. The assessment of internalized homophobic attitudes and beliefs is usually not temporally urgent other than with regard to formation of the therapy alliance. Clients' internalized beliefs are usually manifested in statements that are relatively straightforward, so that, even if attitudes are only occasionally expressed, they should be clear enough to assess.

Therapists may note, for example, relationship problems that come from attitudes of internalized homophobia; examples include devaluing self and others, holding stereotypes about homosexual relationships not lasting, having little hope about conflict resolution, and having a lack of hope or commitment to the gay relationship. Perhaps the most succinct view of themselves that many clients with high internalized homophobia hold is summarized by the word "perverse"; they feel perverse in many ways.

Behaviors as well as attitudes reflecting internalized hate or inferiority are often present, to a varying degree, in gay and lesbian clients. Individuals with lower levels of internalized hate may show more subtle indications of similar beliefs (sometimes hidden to themselves). Attitudes may include a tendency to devalue other gays (perhaps the therapist, if thought or known to be gay), to accept fewer rights for gay and lesbian persons, and to believe that gays are intrinsically less "normal" than heterosexuals.

Clients may believe that they or other lesbians and gay men are not good role models for the children of family or friends. They may think that child care is an inappropriate occupation for homosexuals. Others may accept, without awareness, gays' lack of institutional benefits and mainstream cultural/social inclusion, or may dress against type for reasons of internalized homophobia.

Clients may feel that a gay therapist would be somehow less objective about the acceptability of homosexuality, or should not expect to be found suitable for treating heterosexual couples in therapy, when the reverse in both situations would be unquestioned. Behaviors such as putting blood relatives before a gay/lesbian spouse may become apparent when holiday celebrations, place of residence, definitions of "family" and "home," and so forth are discussed. Clients may see other lesbians and gays as unattractive or less professional and capable in an occupation.

Clients with lower internalized homophobia may have a core sense of themselves that is closer to "different" than "perverse." They are more likely to test or educate the therapist on homophobia, or they may have the confidence to directly demand that the therapist be non-homophobic.

In terms of treatment or intervention, clients with lower levels of internalized homophobia and/or lower levels of trauma in their pasts can often experience decreases in internalized homophobia quickly and with ease. The simplest form of intervention is probably when the therapist points out and questions the implicit homophobic beliefs in a direct manner. Therapists may also identify and challenge behaviors and their sources. The clients with less internalized homophobia will usually respond well to cognitive interventions and reframing.

Clients with a history of past trauma and/or high levels of internalized homophobia may not be able to tolerate a direct challenge, no matter how gentle. For example, these clients might experience verbal comments about their internalized homophobia as one more failure in their individual perceptions and coping abilities. Generally speaking, any intervention that could be perceived as a psychoanalytic interpretation should be cautiously approached.

Progress toward increasing a client's awareness of internalized homophobia will invariably be much slower when the self that struggles with homophobia has otherwise been significantly damaged and compromised. All issues can be worked on simultaneously to some extent in longer-term therapy, and one may observe variations in a client's progress in different parts of their lives, even as overall progress on internalized homophobia seems excruciatingly slow or even nonexistent. One intervention available to the therapist at almost all times is to validate the reality of external oppression when the client expresses some awareness of that reality.

At times, work with clients having both past trauma and internalized homophobia may require an overlapping focus on the two goals of increasing awareness of internal homophobia and increasing awareness of connections between internalized homophobia and the past, and so on. In other words, the therapist might need to define internalized homophobia almost completely as a response to yet more abuse in the client's life. For clients with past trauma, it is probably not helpful to use the term "internalized homophobia" (or any similar term); instead, the therapist should focus the therapy on how all abuse has interacted to oppress the individual.

It may be useful with such clients to deemphasize the power or importance of psychotherapy, both the institution of therapy and the current therapy. The therapist in that case would focus less on homosexuality and therapy, and more on the past and therapy. In this way the connection between being gay and needing therapy is decreased without rejecting the client in his or her request for help.

Increasing Insight into Connections Between Internalized Homophobia and Factors Such As External Stressors, Personal History, and Self-Esteem

The third goal in treating clients with internalized homophobia is to increase their awareness of connections between internal homophobia and past history, current oppression, and personal variables such as self-esteem and self-strength that have helped modulate the effects of the external factors. Clients who more easily become aware of their internalized homophobia will tend to move naturally into an introspective discussion of the source and maintenance of those attitudes. Here the therapist can help the client organize and verbalize ideas. This is probably all that is needed with such clients, but therapists should not encourage a premature endorsement of cause and effect relationships that limit the client's freedom to explore their thoughts and feelings at length.

Work on this goal of integrating connections between internalized homophobia and the past, and so forth, for clients with both low as well as high internalized homophobia, empowers the individual with respect to the critical nature of outside influences such as discrimination and abuse. Clients with high internalized homophobia and/or a history of trauma can also gain a sense of choice in studying the impact of various elements of their lives; without an opportunity to choose among treatment goals, the task of decreasing pain and symptoms could seem to be an overwhelming amount of work. With help in differentiating internalized homophobia from overall self-esteem, the effects of child abuse, current discrimination, and so on, the client can approach psychotherapy with more hope and less self-blame.

CASE STUDIES

The following case illustrations involve two psychotherapy clients, both lesbians. The clients were seen in an outpatient clinic setting for weekly psychotherapy over a period of several months or more. The same psychologist, a woman, saw both clients. The two cases are described regarding how internalized homophobia may interfere with therapy success, such as in achieving the goals identified above, while presenting unique therapeutic opportunities. Names and identifying details have been changed.

Jae

Jae, a white lesbian woman, was twenty-eight years old at the time of the first appointment. She was attractive, yet appeared older than her years. Her physical movements were stiff and self-conscious, and her eye contact was very poor.

She was referred by her family physician, who had followed her through a recent psychiatric admission for depression. Jae had a history of suicide attempts and hospitalizations, and of inconsistent follow-up with psychotherapy. She had seen many therapists since age sixteen, and the longest therapy had been about fifteen appointments over nine months.

Jae's most positive long relationship in her life had been with a great-aunt whom Jae could turn to, in childhood, at times when her parents were especially unavailable. The great-aunt died when Jae was fourteen. Jae had been overweight from early school age until the last two years of high school, when she nearly starved herself in an attempt to become thin. Her earliest weight gain (around six or seven years old) coincided with the onset of sexual abuse by a neighbor, an uncle, and probably others.

Jae had, at different times, been given diagnoses of mixed or borderline personality disorder, post-traumatic stress disorder, alcohol abuse, and depression. She had abused alcohol from her early teens until age twenty-three or so. She said that facing her lesbianism in her early twenties helped her decrease drinking.

Jae did not consider herself a feminist and had little interest in lesbian rights or politics. She was "out" to nearly everyone in her life, including elderly neighbors, co-workers at the automotive plant, and biological family; and on the surface, she seemed to feel and act as if her lesbianism was irrelevant to the rest of her life. There was a matter-of-fact manner in the way Jae and her lesbian friends mixed with heterosexual friends, went to straight as well as gay bars, propositioned apparently straight women, and occasionally slept with gay or straight men.

Jae was in a new relationship with a woman as the therapy began. She said she was in love with this partner and that they had recently moved in together. The therapist speculated that the increased intimacy and commitment in the love relationship had, for Jae, caused some fears and temporary fragmentation, thereby triggering the suicide attempt which had precipitated her most recent hospitalization.

Jae was easy to connect with from the beginning of the therapy, although she acknowledged that "real" trust was very hard for her. A pattern became clear, in which she overtrusted people at first, became hurt and angry over a misunderstanding, then often would end the relationship with a fight. Jae's active and assertive nature and her pattern of quickly connecting and disconnecting with others contributed to numerous physical as well as verbal altercations over the years; most were a result of relationship misunderstandings.

Jae decided, and her referring doctor concurred, that her main goal for the therapy was to keep from "screwing up" her current relationship. The past two hospitalizations had resulted in increased insight into the connection between relationship problems and suicidal threats or attempts.

Although the beginning of the therapy alliance was quickly established, the therapist was aware of the overtrusting dynamic, and took care to obtain a good history in the first two sessions. The therapist felt that Jae had enough potential for insight that, as the inevitable crises came up, she could be helped by a verbal understanding of the fragmenting process. The necessary foundation for such cognitive interventions in crisis would be a solid knowledge of Jae's background that would allow the therapist to point out parallels between the present and her past, to point out the self-soothing and coping strategies she used with more or less success in the past, and to help Jae understand the details of the escalating panic response itself.

The therapist felt that before self-hate issues could be explored, Jae (and the therapist) needed more evidence of her ability to bounce back. Even though high levels of internalized homophobia were evident, it did not appear that Jae could handle painful internal exploration until she was better at recovering from such potentially fragmenting experiences.

The therapist noted signs of internalized hate for later therapeutic use, although it was impossible to differentiate completely the self-hate about being a lesbian from the self-hate for merely existing. However, gay-related self-hate was probably a major cause of Jae's foggy sense of identity as a lesbian and her pessimism about lesbian relationships in general. She did not seem to be curious about the therapist's sexual orientation, and apparently assumed the therapist was heterosexual. She spoke disparagingly of "the gay life" as being debaucherous and hopelessly unhappy.

The therapist initially met with Jae twice per week as needed, then once per week. She focused on helping Jae verbalize her fragmentation in panic-related terms and observe the suicidal feelings that followed the panic. Jae learned to identify what she wanted from her partner and others at that crisis point, even if getting it was technically impossible, and what sort of behaviors on the part of those others escalated the panic. She gained some understanding of how even temporary abandonment was intolerable for her, as was being alone in general. The therapist saw it as not helpful, and probably even harmful at that time, to point out Jae's participation in constructing a rather chaotic life which included the cycle of feeling alone and panicky in the isolation, followed by feeling overinvolved and vulnerable to abandonment, misunderstanding, and so on.

Probably as harmful as too much interpretation would have been too much emphasis on identifying internalized homophobia. Instead the therapist attempted to provide a combination of a space where Jae could be vulnerable without significant attacks resulting, and an emotional and conceptual framework within which she could learn to calm herself.

Jae was able to avoid any other hospitalizations from the beginning of the therapy through the next few years. She was scheduling about two appointments per month by the end of two years. During that time, crisis calls and suicidal impulses gradually decreased.

Virtually no significant disruptions of the therapy relationship occurred during that time, including late cancellations, anger toward the therapist, or otherwise. Jae taught her partner about herself as she learned about the mood swings and her responses to them.

During the third and fourth years of therapy she came in bimonthly or monthly. During the second and later years, Jae occasionally encountered the therapist at large lesbian/gay gatherings. She eagerly spoke to the therapist at such meetings, but seemed to view the new information about the therapist's sexual orientation in much the same way she had previously—as irrelevant.

Jae seemed motivated to keep separate the therapist-client roles and intuitively participated in keeping boundaries that protected the therapy relationship from conflict. Because of this behavior, and because of Jae's more infrequent scheduling after the first two years, the therapist felt that Jae was uninterested or unable to tolerate deeper exploration of past trauma issues at this time. It seemed as if Jae had built for herself (with the therapist's cooperation) a therapy of protection, safety from conflict, and increased stability—one that would be limited at this time to these functions.

Without the support of more frequent scheduling, Jae would probably not have been able to delve more into the older, deeper issues. The therapist felt that Jae would likely be capable of such work sometime in the future. During the therapy, however, Jae did appear to make noticeable progress toward achieving and maintaining a more cohesive self—an important gain.

With reference to the three goals of psychotherapy specifically hypothesized in this report as being useful for clients with internalized homophobia, it seems that Jae made self-strength progress within the context of working on establishing and maintaining/using the therapeutic relationship. The goal of increasing awareness of internalized homophobia was never extensively explored within this piece of therapy, nor was the goal of connecting internalized homophobia and other issues. If and when the therapy continues for Jae, she could be ready for work on those goals together with the depth work probably needed.

Interestingly, by the fourth year of the then-intermittent therapy, Jae showed signs of significantly less internalized homophobia. Her confidence had increased and her self-image seemed slightly more positive. Relationships with lesbian friends were less chaotic and more satisfying, and she expressed fewer and milder statements of self-hate.

It is impossible to specify agents of change, but the therapist speculated that the increased ability to self-soothe led to a greater sense of self-efficacy and thus self-respect. Perhaps the self-respect generalized to Jae's sense of herself as a lesbian. This would suggest that internalized homophobia, for someone with a history of trauma such as Jae, may decrease as a part of building a strong therapy relationship.

Lettie

Lettie, a white divorced woman, entered therapy self-referred. She was thirty-four, had a ten-year-old child, and had recently ended a two-year relationship; it had been her first relationship with a woman.

Lettie said that she had married her husband because of a life-long wish for children, while knowing the marriage would give way eventually to her need to be in a lesbian relationship. The recent breakup led to her seeking therapy. She was aware, through her already extensive contacts with the gay/lesbian community, that the therapist was a lesbian.

Lettie presented as a self-confident, socially adept woman who worked as a paralegal. She described what had been a friendly but nonpassionate marriage, and a childhood with generally positive relationships with parents, sibling, and friends. Her parents divorced when she was twelve, and she described the time between the separation and the final divorce as the hardest time in her life.

Lettie went to brief individual therapy at that age, and attended a group for children with divorcing parents. She expressed her observation that the recent relationship breakup reminded her of those losses she felt when her parents divorced. She stated that her adjustment to her own divorce and to the lesbian relationship that she initiated soon after was easy; she said that she had "ten years of marriage to adjust" to this change.

At the beginning of the therapy, grief issues predominated. After weekly therapy of about three months' duration, Lettie increased the amount of the time that she spent discussing her lesbianism. She started seeing a woman casually, and the pain of the loss lifted a little.

Lettie explored what appeared to be connections between the breakup and increased doubts about her attractiveness to other women and her overall self-image as a lesbian. She recognized as homophobic her feeling that lesbian relationships were somehow inferior or less worthy of rights and respect. It appeared to the therapist that the internalized homophobia had increased dramatically with the loss of the first lesbian relationship.

Lettie talked about her hesitation to introduce her new partner to her straight friends until the partner would dress up, or look "more feminine." She had thought she was unaffected by others' approval, but could now see various ways in which the internalized homophobia surfaced, as the therapist encouraged her to explore the feelings. The therapist assessed, partly based upon the history of generally positive relationships with others, that Lettie was able to accept and integrate occasional challenges to her internalized homophobic attitudes; however, the therapist left the pace and depth of the exploration in Lettie's control.

After several months, Lettie became active in a local lesbian association and developed a strong interest in additional leadership roles. The therapist surmised that Lettie was ready to act on her insights which had significantly reduced her internalized homophobia, and to solidify her increasingly positive lesbian identity by committing to those beliefs in a more public manner. The therapist observed the positive results of this emphasis in therapy on Lettie's understanding and decreased internalized homophobia, as well as in the behaviors and activity that both reinforced, and were reinforced by, the improved self-regard as a lesbian.

CONCLUSION

The two case studies outlined above illustrate a focal model for increasing therapeutic efficacy in clients with internalized homophobia. In the first case, with Jae, the client's process of establishing, maintaining, and eventually using the benefits of a strong therapeutic relationship was the primary goal focused on. The importance of this goal for clients with trauma histories is not restricted to those with internalized homophobia, of course. However, this case illustrates one way in which a client with high internalized homophobia and high-trauma history can be treated effectively, and is consistent with the model proposed.

With Lettie, in the second case, the third goal—that of making connections between internalized homophobia and other issues—was largely put aside because the client felt ready to stop therapy before this part of the work was started. However, Lettie did achieve considerable progress on the first two goals and showed enough introspective ability that her growth on the third goal seemed likely to continue after the therapy, and in fact might not require additional therapy to continue.

The two cases show significant differences in client psychological needs relative to internalized homophobia and therapeutic efficacy. The cases also demonstrate how an understanding of internalized homophobia, when integrated with sound therapeutic methods and sensitivity to the unique psychological needs of each client, can increase the effectiveness of psychotherapy.

REFERENCES

Cabaj, R. P. (1996a). Gay, lesbian, and bisexual mental health professionals and their colleagues. In R. P. Cabaj and T. S. Stein (Eds.), *Textbook of homosexuality and mental health* (pp. 33-42). Washington, DC: American Psychiatric Press, Inc.

Cabaj, R. P. (1996b). Sexual orientation of the therapist. In R. P. Cabaj and T. S. Stein (Eds.), *Textbook of homosexuality and mental health* (pp. 513-524). Washington, DC: American Psychiatric Press, Inc.

Cabaj, R. P. (1996c). Substance abuse in gay men, lesbians, and bisexuals. In R. P. Cabaj and T. S. Stein (Eds.), *Textbook of homosexuality and mental health* (pp. 783-800). Washington, DC: American Psychiatric Press, Inc.

Downey, J. I. and Friedman, R. C. (1996). The negative therapeutic reaction and self-hatred in gay and lesbian patients. In R. P. Cabaj and T. S. Stein (Eds.), *Textbook of homosexuality and mental health* (pp. 471-484). Washington, DC: American Psychiatric Press, Inc.

Falco, K. L. (1996). Psychotherapy with women who love women. In R. P. Cabaj and T. S. Stein (Eds.), *Textbook of homosexuality and mental health* (pp. 397-412). Washington, DC: American Psychiatric Press, Inc.

Gonsiorek, J. C. (1982). The use of diagnostic concepts in working with gay and lesbian populations. *Journal of Homosexuality, 7*(2/3), 9-20.

Gonsiorek, J. C. (1988). Mental health issues of gay and lesbian adolescents. *Journal of Adolescent Health Care, 9*(2), 114-122.

Herek, G. M. (1996). Heterosexism and homophobia. In R. P. Cabaj and T. S. Stein (Eds.), *Textbook of homosexuality and mental health* (pp. 101-114). Washington, DC: American Psychiatric Press, Inc.

Jones, B. E., and Hill, M. J. (1996). African-American lesbians, gay men, and bisexuals. In R. P. Cabaj and T. S. Stein (Eds.), *Textbook of homosexuality and mental health* (pp. 549-562). Washington, DC: American Psychiatric Press, Inc.

Kitzinger, C. (1996). Speaking of oppression: Psychology, politics, and language of power. In E. D. Rothblum and L. A. Bond (Eds.), *Preventing heterosexism and homophobia* (pp. 3-19). Thousand Oaks, CA: Sage Publications, Inc.

Klinger, R. L. (1996). Lesbian couples. In R. P. Cabaj and T. S. Stein (Eds.), *Textbook of homosexuality and mental health* (pp. 339-352). Washington, DC: American Psychiatric Press, Inc.

Klinger, R. L. and Stein, T. S. (1996). Impact of violence, childhood sexual abuse, and domestic violence and abuse on lesbians, bisexuals, and gay men. In R. P. Cabaj and T. S. Stein (Eds.), *Textbook of homosexuality and mental health* (pp. 801-818). Washington, DC: American Psychiatric Press, Inc.

Knisely, E. R. (1992). Psychosocial factors relevant to homosexual men who were sexually abused as children and homosexual men who were not sexually abused as children: An exploratory-descriptive study. *Dissertation Abstracts International, 53*(6): DA9227923.

Malyon, A. K. (1982). Psychotherapeutic implications of internalized homophobia in gay men. *Journal of Homosexuality, 7*(2/3), 59-69.

Nungesser, L. G. (1983). *Homosexual acts, actors, and identities.* New York: Praeger.

Perkins, R. E. (1996). Rejecting therapy: Using our communities. In E. D. Rothblum and L. A. Bond (Eds.), Preventing heterosexism and homophobia (pp. 71-83). Thousand Oaks, CA: Sage Publications, Inc.

Purcell, D. W. and Hicks, D. W. (1996). Institutional discrimination against lesbians, gay men, and bisexuals: The courts, legislature, and the military. In R. P. Cabaj and T. S. Stein (Eds.), *Textbook of homosexuality and mental health* (pp. 763-782). Washington, DC: American Psychiatric Press, Inc.

Ross, M. W. (1996). Societal reaction and homosexuality. In E. D. Rothblum and L. A. Bond (Eds.), *Preventing heterosexism and homophobia* (pp. 211-218). Thousand Oaks, CA: Sage Publications, Inc.

Ross, M. W. and Rosser, B. R. (1996). Measurement and correlates of internalized homophobia: A factor analytic study. *Journal of Clinical Psychology, 52*(1), 15-21.

Seibt, A. C., Ross, M. W., Freeman, A., Krepcho, M., Hedrich, A., McAlister, A., and Fernandez-Esquer, M. E. (1995). Relationship between safe sex and acculturation into the gay subculture. *AIDS Care, 7*(Suppl. 1), S85-S88.

Shidlo, A. (1994). Internalized homophobia: Conceptual and empirical issues in measurement. In B. Greene and G. Herek (Eds.), *Lesbian and gay psychology: Theory, research and clinical applications* (pp. 176-205). Thousand Oaks, CA: Sage.

Sophie, J. (1987). Internalized homophobia and lesbian identity. *Journal of Homosexuality, 14*(1/2), 53-65.

Stein, T. S. (1996). Lesbian, gay, and bisexual families: Issues in psychotherapy. In R. P. Cabaj and T. S. Stein (Eds.), *Textbook of homosexuality and mental health* (pp. 503-512). Washington, DC: American Psychiatric Press, Inc.

Stein, T. S. and Cabaj, R. P. (1996). Psychotherapy with gay men. In R. P. Cabaj and T. S. Stein (Eds.), *Textbook of homosexuality and mental health* (pp. 413-432). Washington, DC: American Psychiatric Press, Inc.

Wagner, G., Brondolo, E., and Rabkin, J. (1996). Internalized homophobia in a sample of HIV+ gay men, and its relationship to psychological distress, coping, and illness progression. *Journal of Homosexuality, 32*(2), 91-106.

Chapter 5

Heterosexist Ideologies and Identity Development: A Transpersonal View

Lynn Pardie

Based upon contemporary research, scholars have become increasingly aware of the complexity and relativity underlying conceptualizations of socioerotic identity (Bohan, 1996; Butler, 1990; D'Augelli, 1994; De Cecco, 1981; De Cecco and Shively, 1983/1984; Gagnon, 1990; Mondimore, 1996). Critical thinking and research indicate (a) that sexual orientation is multiply determined; (b) that the actual vissicitudes of sexual desire are not adequately captured by rigid categories; (c) that there can be variability in erotic experience and sexual expression across the lifespan; and (d) that there are no necessary linkages among physical markers of sex, sexual orientation, and/or personality attributes. Although biological correlates of sexual orientation have been reported and continue to be the focus of some research, social-historical analyses and first-person accounts indicate that the behavioral expression, self-understanding, and social acceptance of one's sexual orientation are significantly affected by the cultural context within which one lives. Clearly, sexual orientation is only one aspect of identity, and knowing whether someone has been erotically attracted to a man, a woman, or both actually tells us very little about that person. And yet, developing a healthy sense of one's socioerotic identity can be difficult for those in the United States who do not fit the heterosex-

The author thanks Barbara Wilson for her very helpful comments on an earlier draft of this chapter.

ual norm because nonheterosexual identities are still stigmatized and extensively marginalized in the dominant culture.

In some ways, continuing opposition to the normative integration of same-sex relationships into mainstream American culture defies logic. More than twenty-five years ago, the American Psychiatric and Psychological Associations officially concluded that a same-sex sexual orientation per se does not reflect mental illness, and accumulated scholarship has unequivocally validated those decisions (see Garnets and Kimmel, 1991; Gonsiorek and Weinrich, 1991; Kurdek, 1994; McLeod and Crawford, 1998; and Patterson, 1994, for reviews). Nevertheless, instances of heterosexist prejudice are visible even within the psychological and psychiatric communities—communities which, by virtue of disciplinary focus, should be most familiar with information about natural diversity in sexual orientation, and about the unnecessary human suffering caused by heterosexism.

In a 1986 survey of psychologists by the American Psychological Association's Committee on Lesbian and Gay Concerns, respondents reported an alarming number of instances in which inadequate knowledge or heterosexist bias among colleagues interfered with the adequate provision of mental health services (Garnets et al., 1991). A small but conspicuous minority of professionals continues to express views depicting same-sex attraction as a symptom of psychopathology or lesser psychological adjustment (e.g., Cameron, Cameron, and Landess, 1996; Nicolosi, 1991; Socarides and Volkan, 1991), evidence to the contrary notwithstanding. Given the difficulty some professionals have had in accepting a normative view of same-sex intimacy, it is little wonder that public attitudes have also shown evidence of misinformation and bias. Studies have shown that many people equate homosexuality with gender nonconformity (Deaux and Lewis, 1984; Herek, 1984; Kite and Deaux, 1987; Taylor, 1983), and some still believe that same-sex relationships are "unnatural," "immoral," or dangerous to society (see Herek, 1991, 1992a, 1992b). The high-profile "don't ask/don't tell" military policy regarding gay and lesbian personnel is a glaring example of the cultural conflict and ambivalence generated by sexual orientation issues. Discrimination and hate crimes against gays and lesbians continue to be significant indicators of the destructive effects of heterosexism and homophobia (Franklin, 1998; Herek and Berrill, 1992).

Negative or biased attitudes toward lesbians and gay men are not just a matter of ignorance regarding naturally occurring variability in sexual orientation. Although anti-gay/lesbian prejudice may represent a variety of underlying motivations at the individual level, such attitudes are primarily empowered and perpetuated at the collective level through deeply held beliefs and values concerning anatomic sex, gender identity and roles, and sexuality (Herek, 1991, 1992a, 1992b; Pharr, 1988; Rothblum and Bond, 1996). To the extent that negative attitudes are a function of deep-seated identity issues and value judgments grounded in a heterosexist worldview, it is unlikely that attitudinal change can be accomplished by merely providing more accurate information about the social construction of gender differences, variability in sexual orientation, or normative features of same-sex relationships. Such information is likely to be rejected when it threatens a sense of personal security and meaning heavily grounded in gender role prescriptions and traditional models of intimate relationships.

In the absence of a pluralistic framework for organizing and comparing perspectives, discussion of heterosexism runs the risk of being regarded as little more than a matter of competing truth claims coming from seemingly unreconcilable worldviews. Therefore, in this chapter, I present an analysis of heterosexism at individual and cultural levels using Ken Wilber's (1995, 1996c) transpersonal meta-theory of spiritual evolution. Wilber's meta-theory provides an integrative framework for comparing worldviews in terms of their psychological, cultural, and historical foundations in relation to spiritual meaning. From a transpersonal perspective, heterosexist views and anti-gay/lesbian attitudes reflect developmental limitations in psychological maturation and spiritual understanding, and changing homonegative attitudes is, at least in part, a matter of transcending traditional conceptions of identity and spirituality.

TRANSPERSONAL PSYCHOLOGY

The transpersonal perspective emerged out of humanistic psychology in the late 1960s in response to growing awareness that some human values and subjective experiences could not be adequately understood using behavioral, psychodynamic, or humanistic frameworks (Valle, 1989). The transpersonal approach, sometimes referred to as the "fourth force" in psychology, uses rational and scientific methodologies to document and conceptualize human experiences and capacities beyond those typical of an ego-identified self. The word *transpersonal* means *beyond the personal*, and transpersonal theorists and researchers seek to understand those individual and collective human experiences more generally referred to as spiritual or beyond the ordinary limits of identity, time, and space. Over the past thirty years, the transpersonal orientation has attracted and influenced researchers and theorists from a variety of academic disciplines, including sociology, anthropology, philosophy, ecology, and psychiatry, as well as psychology (Walsh and Vaughan, 1993).

The most comprehensive transpersonal model has been developed by Wilber (1995, 1996a, 1996b, 1996c, 1998). The model incorporates contemporary research and empirical observation from conventional academic disciplines, as well as from diverse Eastern and Western contemplative traditions and practices. A full description of Wilber's unified theory of spirituality is well beyond the scope of this chapter, and it is strongly suggested that those interested in a deeper understanding of transpersonal meta-theory refer to his original work. However, the following paragraphs provide a brief overview of the transpersonal perspective on psychological development in relation to spiritual meaning.

Spirit is an evolving process emerging in and through physical, biological, and psychological levels of existence (Wilber, 1995, 1996c). Each successive level includes the previous levels, in nested fashion, but reveals new or emergent aspects of existence not present at lower levels. Thus, the psychological realm represents greater depth of Spirit because it transcends, but still includes, the biological and physical realms. Individual spiritual development is understood to be a psychobiological and sociocultural process through which we come to successively deeper and more accurate levels of awareness regarding the nature of existence. It can extend beyond the mature ego-based personality into higher existential and transpersonal states of awareness.

The heart of psychological and spiritual development involves coming to understand and transcend the sharply defined conceptual boundaries which create in-group/out-group tensions and blind us to deeper spiritual connectedness. The human ability to conceptualize and categorize, when coupled with the psychological process of identity formation, has as much power to conceal our sacred commonalities as it does to reveal the diverse expressions of Spirit through our differences. While unlabeled experiences can go unnoticed and unappreciated, labeled experiences can appear static and reified to the point where they seem to have an isolated existence of their own. From a transpersonal perspective, rigid self-concepts which deny the fluid and shared nature of our existence, or conceal the value of spiritual representations falling outside self-referential boundaries, are illusory and immature. Ultimately, the depth of our conscious sense of balance between autonomy and relatedness, as well as our appreciation for spiritual connectedness, will be inversely related to the narrowness and rigidity of our self-definitions.

The conceptual foundations of personal identity are established within the context of a dominant worldview; thus, subjective experience is typically distorted or constrained to some extent by the cultural filter, as well as by the limits of cognitive and emotional development (Wilber, 1986a, 1986b, 1995). The unquestioned introjection of social rules and roles can interfere with genuine self-awareness, limit self-actualization, and create superficial relationships based more on conformity and needs for approval than on authentic being. Relatively greater psychological maturation and spiritual understanding is reflected when aspects of personal identity are grounded in realistically differentiated but relatively flexible identifications. Achieving such an identity depends upon developing mature ego capacities for emotional modulation, formal operational thought, and postconventional modes of moral reasoning, and upon experiencing the motivation to question and move beyond rigid and constraining self-concepts. In order to appreciate sacred commonalities which defy concrete conceptual distinctions, a person must be able to transcend egocentric and sociocentric concerns, and adopt a more neutral pluralistic perspective.

HETEROSEXISM: REDUCTIONISTIC AND POLARIZING IDENTIFICATIONS

Sex, sexuality, sexual orientation, and *gender,* as psychological constructions, represent related conceptual systems. They reflect categories which are intended to capture and differentiate essential features of certain forms of experience. However, their definitional boundaries must be regarded as relatively fluid and evolving because psychological meanings are always situated in particular socioeconomic, cultural, and historical contexts. The categories exist as conceptual frameworks that influence and are influenced by worldviews. From a transpersonal perspective, the experiences represented by such constructions are multifaceted, and include objective and subjective aspects in individual and collective dimensions. For example, sexuality is a category system representing those thoughts, feelings, and behaviors which have erotic meaning in both intrapersonal and interpersonal dimensions. Such experiences comprise biological and psychological/cultural levels. Each level reveals its own form of truth or meaning about sexuality; although there are objectively observable facts regarding biological and behavioral aspects of sexuality, sexual expression also reveals psychological truths and cultural meanings which cannot be legitimately reduced to biological or behavioral facts. Such meanings are context-bound, and can be known only through subjective awareness and interpersonal communication.

Along parallel lines, the phenomenal experiences we seek to capture with the category systems of sex, gender, and sexual orientation also exist at multiple levels of reference (e.g., biology versus psychology), and involve objectively observable and subjective dimensions (e.g., behavior versus psychological intent). Sex refers to the categorization of individuals as male or female based on biological or anatomical markers, and is not synonymous with the socially constructed meanings of gender. Although sex, sexual orientation, and gender appear to represent discrete categories (i.e., male/female, heterosexual/homosexual/bisexual, or masculine/feminine), rigid conceptual distinctions can hide the more fluid and flexible nature of actual experience. The behaviors, characteristics, and meanings typically associated with particular categories of gender and sexual orientation have been found to vary across historical periods and cultures (Greenberg, 1988; Katz, 1995; Weinrich and Williams, 1991), and individual erotic experience can vary across the life span (Blumstein and Schwartz, 1990; Golden, 1987; Rust, 1996).

In contrast to this multifaceted and more flexible understanding, the heterosexist worldview which typically underlies homonegative attitudes represents a system of beliefs and expectations regarding sex-specific characteristics, interests, roles, sexual values, and relational dynamics (Herek, 1992a; Rose, 1996). Traditional marriage models have been grounded in power differences favoring men and in expectations for complementary relational behaviors based on polarized gender prescriptions (Eisler, 1995; Foucault, 1978-1986). Despite periodic variations in sexual interests and mores, exclusive definitions of *family* based on kinship suggest that sexual and relational behaviors have been collectively valued primarily for their reproductive and economic potentials. Heterosexual relationships are privileged legally, socially, and in language. Such perspectives, emerging in part through Judeo-Christian religious mythologies and traditions, have significantly shaped prevailing conceptions of what it means to be a man or woman in our culture, as well as what constitutes a morally valuable, socially acceptable, sexually intimate relationship.

Sociocultural and Historical Origins of Heterosexism

Although some might claim that a heterosexist worldview occurs naturally rather than through social conditioning, research indicates that children begin to make sex-linked differentiations around age two, and that the complex cognitive process of linking anatomical sex to specific cognitive, emotional, and behavioral aspects of experience continues through adolescence (Bem, 1981; Fagot, 1995; Huston and Alvarez, 1990). Developing children incorporate dominant ideologies regarding gender and sexuality into their identities and expectations of others through passive exposure to cultural messages, as well as through active conditioning by significant others. Physical activities are often sex-segregated. Girls and boys learn to be differentially sensitive to metacommunication messages regarding relational connectedness and hierarchical status (Wood, 1994). They are also likely to develop different levels of comfort with sexual behavior, different schemas of meaning regarding sexual behavior, and different sexual scripts based on gender roles (Tiefer and Kring, 1995), despite the potential relationship difficulties differential socialization might cause.

Transpersonal theory synthesizes an enormous body of scholarship which indicates that the development of individual identities and the evolution of collective cultures show significant parallels in developmental sequencing and form (Wilber, 1995, 1996a, 1996b, 1996c). Culture is understood as a collective expression of the dominant beliefs, assumptions, and values that make experience meaningful and seemingly more predictable. It is transmitted as younger members of society are taught to view the world according to prevailing guidelines. However, assumptions underlying the dominant culture reflect whatever psychological, social, and environmental constraints are in effect at that particular point in history. The persistence of particular worldviews depends as much on their power to provide meaning and comfort to members of society as on their factual fit with reality. Because current constructions of sexuality and gender have been shaped, at least in part, through Judeo-Christian mythologies, it is important to consider the psychological limitations which constrained the original mythological worldviews themselves.

Contemporary psychological templates for gender and sexuality can be traced back to distinctions originally based on reproductive and strength-related work roles (Chafetz, 1984; Eisler, 1987, 1995; Lorber, 1994). According to Eisler, evidence of power distortions and the differential valuing of men and women were not consistently found among early civilizations. When significant value differences emerged, they probably arose in specific social groupings, as a function of sex-linked divisions of labor necessitated by the survival demands of particular geographic, climatic, and technological conditions. Stereotypic masculine images, which devalue emotional sensitivity but emphasize physical prowess and aggressive competition, have been linked to the need for killing as a means of food production, group competition for scarce resources, and physical defense. Along similar lines, stereotypic feminine images parallel the functional demands of child-rearing and home-related tasks. In short, a number of biological, physical, and environmental factors shaped evolving conceptualizations of the "natural" world for early human groups, and these unquestioned patterns would eventually form biologically and socially embedded foundations for identity.

According to Wilber (1995, 1996c), men and women were most strongly defined by sex-specific roles during the late mythic period of human evolution (roughly 4500-1500 B.C.E.), and this is the period from which many religious belief systems have evolved. Mythologies represented human attempts to make sense of existence, and were marked by particular psychological and social characteristics. Research suggests that, in the later mythic period, modal levels of cognitive development were largely limited to concrete reasoning and conventional forms of moral judgment (see Wilber, 1995, 1996a, 1996b, for supporting research). Reality was generally understood in an egocentric and literal way. Concrete reasoning provides no conceptual basis for making distinctions between what occurs in the world and what should occur, so existing sex-linked divisions of labor and power differences were probably understood to be "natural," and therefore moral, imperatives.

When shared by people of different blood lineages and kinship origins, mythologies enabled the rise of larger integrated societies and introduced problems of social control. Sociocentric or ethnocentric concerns for survival and prosperity generated social hierarchies of roles and rules, which were believed to be divinely ordained by one or more gods. Group identification and belongingness needs allowed for the development of a morality based on shared values and social conformity. Individual responsibility was a matter of obedience to established rules.

Mythic societies were generally governed, in authoritarian fashion, by men who derived political power through their functional relationship to mythic gods. Although the deities were projected archetypal images of humans, the power attributed to them provided a sense of safety and security to those who conformed to established rules. Conflicting mythological worldviews typically resulted in wars since proponents of different mythic belief systems felt empowered and required, by the divine will of respective gods, to impose their worldview on others.

Wilber (1995, 1996b, 1996c) refers to this developmental level of covarying individual and collective consciousness as *mythic-membership* organization. Identities so constructed were developmentally and spiritually limited in terms of genuine self-awareness and relational depth because they were socially, and to some extent biologically, embedded. Concrete reasoning and needs for security and belongingness generated a conceptual self fundamentally grounded in sex differences, group memberships, and social scripts for conformity. Membership identities essentially represented conscious personae, or socially conditioned masks, based on differing group affiliations and social roles. Primitive psychological defenses enabled the unconscious projection of forbidden thoughts and impulses, so that the social world appeared to be grounded in sharply defined in-group/out-group distinctions typically representing "good" conformists and "evil" nonconformists. Some of the developmental constraints of mythic-membership thinking influenced subsequent psychological and cultural development; such development would be marked by the further separation of experience into isolated material and spiritual domains (i.e., the visible world versus other-worldly projections), and by a heterosexual relational model predicated on sex-linked power differences and distorted views of women and sexuality.

Contemporary Remnants of Mythic-Membership Views

As the structures of consciousness have evolved, increasing capacities for emotional control, formal operational thought, and post-conventional moral reasoning have allowed awareness to emerge more fully from biological and social embeddedness, and to include greater appreciation of and respect for individuality (Wilber, 1995, 1996b). At the sociocultural level, such capacities have enabled the development of societies based on more democratic and pluralistic ideals rather than on egocentric or ethnocentric concerns blind to common bonds in Spirit. Thus, there is the potential for transcending polarized gender expectations and for becoming more aware of shared psychological attributes and deeper relational values. However, Wilber also argues that large segments of the world's population continue to rationalize divisive, mythologically based, religious beliefs and to experience themselves and others in terms of in-group/out-group distinctions.

With regard to heterosexism, it seems clear that the developmentally limited perspective which gave rise to repressive and reductionistic beliefs in Judeo-Christian mythologies continues to constrain many individuals' understanding of sexuality, gender, and relationship. Despite the legal separation of church and state, aspects of both mythic and rational structures continue to inform contemporary culture and social institutions within the United States. We have inherited an extensive institutionalized system of providing interpersonal acknowledgment and support which focuses, almost exclusively, on heterosexual marriage and a kinship model of family.

In the dominant worldview, our expectations of the flow of life and our ability to see and meet needs for support during stressful life events are largely filtered through the heterosexual marriage and family model (Herek, 1992a; Slater, 1995). Through it, we learn to anticipate some of the life events that may threaten the well-being of a married couple's relationship, and to provide encouragement and support to the partners during times of such stress. The legal recognition of heterosexual marriage is a formal acknowledgment of the socioeconomic value assigned to this form of relationship; the partners' access to each other and to mutually developed assets is seen as worthy of special protection.

In stark contrast, similar social and legal valuing is not readily available for gay and lesbian couples, no matter how closely entwined their daily lives and finances, no matter how deep their commitment to each other, no matter how willing they are to engage in shared parenting or elder care. The psychological and spiritual significance of intimate same-sex relationships is virtually unrecognized by the dominant culture because such relationships transcend traditional conceptualizations of gender complementarity and sexuality which form the core of heterosexual identities and relational models. This is a clear example of the destructive downside of some worldviews; they can conceal as much of value as they reveal to us.

Developmental Parallels with Homonegative Attitudes

A number of factors associated with negative attitudes toward lesbians and gay men parallel the developmental limitations of a mythic-membership perspective. Generally speaking, individuals who express negative attitudes tend (a) to have repressive views on sexuality (Herek, 1984); (b) to endorse stereotypic gender roles (Kite and Deaux, 1987; Newman, 1989; Whitley, 1987); (c) to exhibit a less mature style of reasoning marked by simplistic categorical dichotomies (Gannon, 1999); (d) to score high on measures of authoritarianism (Herek, 1984; Haddock and Zanna, 1998); and (e) to be actively involved in conservative or fundamentalist religious groups emphasizing literal interpretations of religious precepts (Herek, 1984, 1987a, 1991; Kirkpatrick, 1993). Such findings strongly suggest the presence of reductionistic and polarized views of men and women, as well as a value orientation grounded in hierarchical relationships and conformity to group norms.

Herek (1987b) has also shown that expressing negative attitudes toward gay men and lesbians can serve identity-reinforcing or self-protective functions; this, too, would be consistent with the approval needs underlying a membership-based identity. When maintaining a secure identity is heavily dependent on receiving external validation for in-group belongingness, publicly conforming to socially and/or religiously defined roles and rules of acceptability becomes very important. Expressing homonegative attitudes creates distance between oneself and a nonconforming group. For those who associate same-sex attraction with gender nonconformity and the violation of sexual mores, expressing anti-gay/lesbian attitudes may reinforce the sense of their own gender "normalcy" and imply moral superiority. When similar beliefs and values are shared by one's support system, the expression of negative attitudes can seem to affirm the prejudicial worldview, as well as the sense of belongingness to the in-group.

For some individuals, prejudice also serves to ward off any uncomfortable personal awareness of same-sex erotic feelings or gender atypical interests and values. The "good" self-concept, grounded in heterosexist parameters, is again protected by establishing a clear boundary line, through repression or suppression, between oneself and everything one associates with homosexuality, whether the associations are valid or not. Lack of deeper self-awareness and ego strength can also lead to defensive projection of unacceptable aspects of one's own personality, so that individuals thought to be homosexual inadvertently serve as the displaced focus for unconscious identity conflicts and hostility. In extreme cases, group identifications, driven by a sense of religious or moral superiority, are ironically linked to destructive hatred and/or violence (Herek and Berrill, 1992).

Certainly, these parallels do not mean that everyone holding Jewish or Christian religious views is heterosexist or homophobic, nor do they mean that all heterosexual relationships are marked by gender stereotypic roles or authoritarian dynamics; clearly that is not the case. From a transpersonal perspective, interpretations of myths will vary considerably depending upon the interpreter's level of psychological maturation, sense of shared humanity, and capacities for formal reasoning and empathy. In fact, some very thoughtful critiques of heterosexism have been written from Christian perspectives which transcend the literal interpretive style of fundamentalism (e.g., Bawer, 1997; Helminiak, 1994; Jung and Smith, 1993).

Nevertheless, it seems logical to assume that more realistic and flexible conceptualizations of gender, sexuality, and relationship will be particularly threatening for individuals who understand themselves and the world through literal or near literal interpretations of Christian or Jewish mythologies. For such individuals, experiencing a continuing sense of meaningfulness in life is contingent on complying with ancient prescriptions which separate men and women according to reproductive and social roles, subjugate women through relational models based on male authority, and repressively control and devalue sexuality.

Transcending Heterosexism: Reaching Deeper Levels of Sexual and Relational Meaning

Unfortunately, the cognitively limited associations and presumptions which differentially linked physical markers of sex to economic roles and social values, and isolated sexuality from its deeper relational and spiritual meanings, have become firmly established as the "natural order" in the dominant worldview. Under stereotypic heterosexual and gender role pressures, relationships may be driven—not by genuine self-awareness, mutuality, and freely given respect—but by established rules of sexual behavior, role reciprocity, and/or submission to authority. Cultural conditioning based on the dominant worldview is powerful. The overwhelming majority of individuals who grow up in the United States develop a sense of self shaped directly or indirectly by heterosexist views. Such views may or may not be consciously tied to fundamentalist religious beliefs. Even the process of healthy identity formation for gay men and lesbians typically involves awakening to internalized hetero-sexism and homonegativity.

From a transpersonal perspective, heterosexist ideologies of gender, sexuality, and relationship represent a formidable obstacle to continued psychological and spiritual maturation when they serve as the foundation for personal identity. They reflect the reification of polarized gender prescriptions and the failure to differentiate biological and psychological aspects of sexuality and relationship. Such thinking limits genuine self-awareness, as well as the experiential basis for appreciating and empathizing with others. Natural variation in sexual orientation and/or in the actual experiences of erotic attraction across the lifespan are obscured by the sharply defined boundaries of stereotypic categories. Variations in sexual intentions and relational meanings are obscured by a reductionistic emphasis on biological reproduction as the only legitimate purpose for sexual relationships. Maintaining a self-image congruent with heterosexual stereotypes requires the psychological distancing of thoughts, feelings, or interests inconsistent with social prescriptions.

Psychological and spiritual growth lies in the direction of transcending the in-group/out-group boundaries we draw between ourselves and others, of opening to the full spectrum of experience and meaning, and of increasing appreciation for the diversity of Spirit. For those whose identities are firmly rooted in a heterosexist worldview, such growth involves consciously suspending judgmental tendencies; disidentifying with stereotypic heterocentric beliefs long enough to question the underlying assumptions and consequences; and developing a more realistic and differentiated understanding of gender, sexual orientation, and sexuality. It also involves looking deeper into the reality of one's own experience of interpersonal attraction, and reconsidering sexual values and relationship dynamics in one's own life. The purpose of such an exploration is not to question the validity of a self-congruent heterosexual orientation, but rather to open awareness to the more subtle dimensions of personal experience and meaning which lie beyond social conditioning. An identity constructed on this more rational and realistic basis is defined by greater authenticity, as well as greater respect for the authentic being of others despite differences. The outcome is greater sensitivity to and appreciation for relational truth, beauty, and goodness—whether expressed through same-sex or other-sex intimacy.

Scholarship regarding the coming out process for lesbians and gay men is consistent with the transpersonal view of identity development. Coming out involves disidentifying with socially conditioned worldviews which do not fit the truth and meaning of subjective experience. The unpredictable circumstances of the journey are such that one is forced to look carefully and openly at one's life experience for the seeds of a more authentic identity—an identity which will be constructed from the truth of one's own interests and preferences, gender stereotypic or not, and of one's own attractions, heterosexual or not. The process is not necessarily an easy one. Coming out generally involves (a) learning to trust the truth of one's erotic experience; (b) confronting fears of change, as well as feelings of shame which have been conditioned to follow violation of heterosexual norms; (c) letting go of relationship scripts rigidly confined to heterosexual images and hierarchical roles and rules; (d) grieving the loss of enculturated heterosexual images of self; and (e) developing a more authentic sense of self (D'Augelli, 1994; Gonsiorek and Rudolph, 1991; Minton and McDonald, 1983/1984; O'Neill and Ritter, 1992). It can also involve awakening to deeper spiritual meanings and values regarding sexuality and relationship—meanings and values which emphasize mutuality, respect, choice, and an intimacy that preserves but also transcends individuality.

THE UNCERTAINTY OF SPIRITUAL DEVELOPMENT: QUESTIONS OF MOTIVATION AND ABILITY

Clearly, gay men and lesbians are deeply and intrinsically motivated to develop beyond heterosexist conformity. Incongruities between heterocentric models of relationship and their own erotic attractions and relational needs and strengths compel lesbians and gay men to question the assumptions underlying gender stereotypes and heterosexual scripts, and to grapple with an extended identity formation process. By contrast, the developmental parameters of heterosexist perspectives and the characteristics associated with the expression of anti-gay/lesbian attitudes suggest that it may be particularly difficult for some heterosexuals to even consider the need for such reflection. Indeed, there are a number of factors that make it less likely that individuals who strongly endorse negative attitudes toward lesbians and gay men will be moved to question core assumptions underlying their own identities.

To question the validity of a heterosexist worldview is to invite the loss of privileges and social prestige differentially associated with being heterosexual in our society. At deeper levels, it involves confronting identity-related anxieties, taboos regarding sexuality, and the historical origins of social customs and religious beliefs which so many take for granted. The possibility of having prematurely foreclosed on one's own identity can arouse deep personal anxiety and stimulate a renewed sense of identity confusion. When compulsory heterosexuality and gender stereotypes are no longer the necessary confines of a spiritually meaningful socioerotic identity, one is opened to an inner and outer space of relational possibilities, erotic and nonerotic, which did not exist from the perspective of the old worldview. As with lesbians and gay men, the impact of this opening promises to be nothing less than an existential challenge.

For those whose worldview is more strongly grounded in fundamentalist religious beliefs, the real world of expanded socioerotic possibilities is especially likely to appear, at least at first, as more chaotic and threatening than the ordered hierarchies prescribed by demanding but protective father-gods, who promised life after death in exchange for compliance. Losing the sense of security and certainty which accompanies such worldviews can precipitate a period of transitional grief and mourning, and trigger a deep psychological struggle with meaninglessness in life. Although such existential struggles with spiritual meaning hold the promise of greater self-awareness, personal freedom, and interpersonal understanding upon transcendent resolution, the developmental constraints which create mythic-membership forms of identity will make that promise incomprehensible to some individuals.

It is likely that those heterosexuals who seriously undertake the challenge are moved to do so out of compassionate concern and/or a desire for greater truthfulness with themselves and others. Traditional gender roles and marriage models have been increasingly questioned by heterosexual men and women because such prescriptions seriously limit the possibilities for true individuality and intimacy in heterosexual relationships. Others have undoubtedly struggled with heterosexist beliefs in an effort to preserve their relationships with family members or friends who are gay or lesbian. In any event, whether motivated by a desire for understanding, or a greater sense of relatedness, or simple compassionate concern, individual struggles to overcome heterosexism have significant psychological and spiritual implications.

Ultimately, the ideologies underlying heterosexism devalue all relationships. Sexuality is neither separate from nor antithetical to Spirit, and the sacred nature of any form of sexual expression is better represented by the depths of relational meaning and spiritual values enacted than by the anatomical sex of the participants or the potential for biological reproduction. Sexual behavior that is freely and consciously chosen, egalitarian in nature, mutually respectful, mutually pleasurable, and mutually caring honors sacred relational qualities which cannot be legitimately reduced to reproductive potential, or to social roles that serve the economic and political goals of particular groups. However, to fully appreciate this truth, one must be willing and able to move beyond an identity constructed in accordance with heterosexist worldviews. The ideologies which create heterosexism are seriously fettered by categorical assumptions and prejudices that interfere with self-actualization, relational creativity, and spiritual understanding. From a transpersonal perspective, our power to create egalitarian and intimate relationships—relationships that honor the verifiable richness and depths of spiritual meaning revealed by reason and awareness—depends upon transcending these limitations.

REFERENCES

Bawer, B. (1997). *Stealing Jesus: How fundamentalism betrays Christianity.* New York: Crown.

Bem, S. L. (1981). Gender schema theory: A cognitive account of sex typing. *Psychological Review, 88*(4), 354-364.

Blumstein, P. and Schwartz, P. (1990). Intimate relationships and the creation of sexuality. In D. P. McWhirter, S. A. Sanders, and J. M. Reinisch (Eds.), *The Kinsey Institute series: Volume 2. Homosexuality/heterosexuality: Concepts of sexual orientation* (pp. 307-320). New York: Oxford University Press.

Bohan, J. S. (1996). *Psychology and sexual orientation: Coming to terms.* New York: Routledge.

Butler, J. P. (1990). *Gender trouble: Feminism and the subversion of identity.* New York: Routledge.

Cameron, P., Cameron, K., and Landess, T. (1996). Errors by the American Psychiatric Association, the American Psychological Association, and the National Educational Association in representing homosexuality in amicus briefs about Amendment 2 to the U. S. Supreme Court. *Psychological Reports, 79*(2), 383-404.

Chafetz, J. S. (1984). *Sex and advantage.* Totowa, NJ: Rowman and Allanheld.

D'Augelli, A. R. (1994). Identity development and sexual orientation: Toward a model of lesbian, gay, and bisexual development. In E. J. Trickett, R. J. Watts, and D. Birman (Eds.), *Human diversity: Perspectives on people in context* (pp. 312-333). San Francisco: Jossey-Bass.

Deaux, K. and Lewis, L. L. (1984). Structure of gender stereotypes: Interrelationships among components and gender label. *Journal of Personality and Social Psychology, 46*(5), 991-1004.

De Cecco, J. P. (1981). Definition and meaning of sexual orientation. *Journal of Homosexuality, 6*(4), 51-67.

De Cecco, J. P. and Shively, M. G. (1983/1984). From sexual identity to sexual relationships: A contextual shift. *Journal of Homosexuality, 9*(2/3), 1-26.

Eisler, R. (1987). *The chalice and the blade: Our history, our future.* New York: HarperCollins.

Eisler, R. (1995). *Sacred pleasure: Sex, myth, and the politics of the body.* New York: HarperCollins.

Fagot, B. I. (1995). Psychosocial and cognitive determinants of early gender-role development. In R. C. Rosen, C. M. Davis, and H. J. Ruppel, Jr. (Eds.), *Annual review of sex research: Volume 6.* (pp. 1-31). Mount Vernon, IA: Society for the Scientific Study of Sexuality.

Foucault, M. (1978-1986). *The history of sexuality* (Volumes 1-3, R. Hurley, Trans.). New York: Random House. (Original work published 1976, 1984).

Franklin, K. (1998). Unassuming motivations: Contextualizing the narratives of antigay assailants. In G.M. Herek (Ed.), *Psychological perspectives on lesbian and gay issues: Volume 4. Stigma and sexual orientation: Understanding prejudice against lesbians, gay men, and bisexuals* (pp. 1-23). Thousand Oaks, CA: Sage.

Gagnon, J. H. (1990). Gender preference in erotic relations: The Kinsey Scale and sexual scripts. In D. P. McWhirter, S. A. Sanders, and J. M. Reinisch (Eds.), *The Kinsey Institute series: Volume 2. Homosexuality/heterosexuality: Concepts of sexual orientation* (pp. 177-207). New York: Oxford University Press.

Gannon, L. (1999). Homphobia in academia: Examination and critique. In L. Pardie and T. Luchetta (Eds.), *The construction of attitudes toward lesbians and gay men* (pp. 43-63). Binghamton, NY: The Haworth Press.

Garnets, L., Hancock, K. A., Cochran, S. D., Goodchilds, J., and Peplau, L. A. (1991). Issues in psychotherapy with lesbians and gay men: A survey of psychologists. *American Psychologist, 46*(9), 964-972.

Garnets, L. and Kimmel, D. (1991). Lesbian and gay male dimensions in the psychological study of human diversity. In J. D. Goodchilds (Ed.), *Psychological perspectives on human diversity in America* (pp. 137-192). Washington, DC: American Psychological Association.

Golden, C. (1987). Diversity and variability in women's sexual identities. In The Boston Lesbian Psychologies Collective (Ed.), *Lesbian psychologies: Explorations and challenges* (pp. 19-34). Urbana, IL: University of Illinois Press.

Gonsiorek, J. C. and Rudolph, J. R. (1991). Homosexual identity: Coming out and other developmental events. In J. C. Gonsiorek and J. D. Weinrich (Eds.), *Homosexuality: Research implications for public policy* (pp. 161-176). Newbury Park, CA: Sage.

Gonsiorek, J. C. and Weinrich, J. D. (Eds.). (1991). *Homosexuality: Research implications for public policy.* Newbury Park, CA: Sage.

Greenberg, D. F. (1988). *The construction of homosexuality.* Chicago: The University of Chicago Press.

Haddock, G. and Zanna, M. P. (1998). Authoritarianism, values, and the favorability and structure of antigay attitudes. In G.M. Herek (Ed.), *Psychological perspectives on lesbian and gay issues: Volume 4. Stigma and sexual orientation: Understanding prejudice against lesbians, gay men, and bisexuals* (pp. 82-107). Thousand Oaks, CA: Sage.

Helminiak, D. A. (1994). *What the Bible really says about homosexuality.* San Francisco: Alamo Square Press.

Herek, G. M. (1984). Beyond "homophobia": A social psychological perspective on attitudes toward lesbians and gay men. *Journal of Homosexuality, 10*(1/2), 1-21.

Herek, G. M. (1987a). Religious orientation and prejudice: A comparison of racial and sexual attitudes. *Personality and Social Psychology Bulletin, 13*(1), 34-44.

Herek, G. M. (1987b). Can functions be measured? A new perspective on the functional approach to attitudes. *Social Psychology Quarterly, 50*(4), 285-303.

Herek, G. M. (1991). Stigma, prejudice, and violence against lesbians and gay men. In J. C. Gonsiorek and J. D. Weinrich (Eds.), *Homosexuality: Research implications for public policy* (pp. 60-80). Newbury Park, CA: Sage.

Herek, G. M. (1992a). The social context of hate crimes: Notes on cultural heterosexism. In G. M. Herek and K. T. Berrill (Eds.), *Hate crimes: Confronting violence against lesbians and gay men* (pp. 89-104). Newbury Park, CA: Sage.

Herek, G. M. (1992b). Psychological heterosexism and anti-gay violence: The social psychology of bigotry and bashing. In G. M. Herek and K. T. Berrill (Eds.), Hate crimes: Confronting violence against lesbians and gay men (pp. 149-169). Newbury Park, CA: Sage.

Herek, G. M. and Berrill, K. T. (Eds.). (1992). *Hate crimes: Confronting violence against lesbians and gay men.* Newbury Park, CA: Sage.

Huston, A. C. and Alvarez, M. M. (1990). The socialization context of gender role development in early adolescence. In R. Montemayor, G. R. Adams, and T. P. Gullotta (Eds.), *Advances in adolescent development: Volume 2. From childhood to adolescence: A transitional period?* (pp. 156-179). Newbury Park, CA: Sage.

Jung, P. B. and Smith, R. F. (1993). *Heterosexism: An ethical challenge.* Albany, NY: State University of New York Press.

Katz, J. N. (1995). *The invention of heterosexuality.* New York: Dutton.

Kirkpatrick, L. A. (1993). Fundamentalism, Christian orthodoxy, and intrinsic religious orientation as predictors of discriminatory attitudes. *Journal for the Scientific Study of Religion, 32*(3), 256-268.

Kite, M. E. and Deaux, K. (1987). Gender belief systems: Homosexuality and the implicit inversion theory. *Psychology of Women Quarterly, 11*(1), 83-96.

Kurdek, L. A. (1994). The nature and correlates of relationship quality in gay, lesbian, and heterosexual cohabiting couples: A test of the individual difference, interdependence, and discrepancy model. In B. Greene and G. M. Herek (Eds.), *Psychological perspectives on lesbian and gay issues: Volume 1. Lesbian and gay psychology: Theory, research, and clinical applications* (pp. 133-155). Thousand Oaks, CA: Sage.

Lorber, J. (1994). *Paradoxes of gender.* New Haven, CT: Yale University Press.

McLeod, A. and Crawford, I. (1998). The postmodern family: An examination of the psychosocial and legal perspectives of gay and lesbian parenting. In G.M. Herek (Ed.), *Psychological perspectives on lesbian and gay issues: Volume 4. Stigma and sexual orientation: Understanding prejudice against lesbians, gay men, and bisexuals* (pp. 211-222). Thousand Oaks, CA: Sage.

Minton, H. L. and McDonald, G. J. (1983/1984). Homosexual identity formation as a developmental process. *Journal of Homosexuality, 9*(2/3), 91-104.

Mondimore, F. M. (1996). *A natural history of homosexuality.* Baltimore, MD: The Johns Hopkins University Press.

Newman, B. S. (1989). The relative importance of gender role attitudes to male and female attitudes toward lesbians. *Sex Roles, 21*(7/8), 451-465.

Nicolosi, J. (1991). *Reparative therapy of male homosexuality.* Northvale, NJ: Jason Aronson.

O'Neill, C. and Ritter, K. (1992). *Coming out within: Stages of spiritual awakening for lesbians and gay men.* New York: HarperCollins.

Patterson, C. J. (1994). Children of the lesbian baby boom: Behavioral adjustment, self-concepts, and sex role identity. In B. Greene and G. M. Herek (Eds.), *Psychological perspectives on lesbian and gay issues: Volume 1. Lesbian and gay psychology: Theory, research, and clinical applications* (pp. 156-175). Thousand Oaks, CA: Sage.

Pharr, S. (1988). *Homophobia: A weapon of sexism.* Inverness, CA: Chardon.

Rose, S. (1996). Lesbian and gay love scripts. In E. D. Rothblum and L. A. Bond (Eds.), *Preventing heterosexism and homophobia* (pp. 151-173). Thousand Oaks, CA: Sage.

Rothblum, E. D. and Bond, L. A. (Eds.). (1996). *Preventing heterosexism and homophobia.* Thousand Oaks, CA: Sage.

Rust, P. C. (1996). Finding a sexual identity and community: Therapeutic implications and cultural assumptions in scientific models of coming out. In E. D. Rothblum and L. A. Bond (Eds.), *Preventing heterosexism and homophobia* (pp. 87-123). Thousand Oaks, CA: Sage.

Slater, S. (1995). *The lesbian family life cycle.* New York: The Free Press.

Socarides, C. W. and Volkan, V. D. (Eds.). (1991). *The homosexualities and the therapeutic process.* Madison, CT: International Universities Press.

Taylor, A. (1983). Conceptions of masculinity and femininity as a basis for stereotypes of male and female homosexuals. *Journal of Homosexuality, 9*(1), 37-53.

Tiefer, L. and Kring, B. (1995). Gender and the organization of sexual behavior. Special issue: Clinical Sexuality. *The Psychiatric Clinics of North America, 18*(1), 25-37.

Valle, R. S. (1989). The emergence of transpersonal psychology. In R. S. Valle and S. Halling (Eds.), *Existential-phenomenological perspectives in psychology: Exploring the breadth of human experience* (pp. 257-268). New York: Plenum.

Walsh, R. and Vaughan, F. (Eds.). (1993). *Paths beyond ego: The transpersonal vision.* New York: Tarcher/Putnam.

Weinrich, J. D. and Williams, W. L. (1991). Strange customs, familiar lives: Homosexualities in other cultures. In J. C. Gonsiorek and J. D. Weinrich (Eds.), *Homosexuality: Research implications for public policy* (pp. 44-59). Newbury Park, CA: Sage.

Whitley, B. E., Jr. (1987). The relationship of sex-role orientation to heterosexuals' attitudes toward homosexuals. *Sex Roles, 17*(1/2), 103-113.

Wilber, K. (1986a). The spectrum of development. In K. Wilber, J. Engler, and D. P. Brown (Eds.), *Transformations of consciousness: Conventional and contemplative perspectives on development* (pp. 65-105). Boston: Shambhala.

Wilber, K. (1986b). The spectrum of psychopathology. In K. Wilber, J. Engler, and D. P. Brown (Eds.), *Transformations of consciousness: Conventional and contemplative perspectives on development* (pp. 107-126). Boston: Shambhala.

Wilber, K. (1995). *Sex, ecology, spirituality: The spirit of evolution.* Boston: Shambhala.

Wilber, K. (1996a). *The atman project: A transpersonal view of human development* (Second edition). Wheaton, IL: Quest Books.

Wilber, K. (1996b). *Up from Eden: A transpersonal view of human evolution* (Second edition). Wheaton, IL: Quest Books.

Wilber, K. (1996c). *A brief history of everything.* Boston: Shambhala.

Wilber, K. (1998). *The marriage of sense and soul: Integrating science and religion.* New York: Random House.

Wood, J. T. (1994). *Gendered lives: Communication, gender, and culture.* Belmont, CA: Wadsworth.

Index

Page numbers followed by the letter "n" indicate notes; those followed by the letter "t" indicate tables.

Order Your Own Copy of
This Important Book for Your Personal Library!

THE CONSTRUCTION OF ATTITUDES TOWARD LESBIANS AND GAY MEN

_____ in hardbound at $29.95 (ISBN: 0-7890-0590-5)

_____ in softbound at $14.95 (ISBN: 1-56023-942-5)

COST OF BOOKS_____

OUTSIDE USA/CANADA/ MEXICO: ADD 20%_____

POSTAGE & HANDLING_____
(US: $3.00 for first book & $1.25 for each additional book)
Outside US: $4.75 for first book & $1.75 for each additional book)

SUBTOTAL_____

IN CANADA: ADD 7% GST_____

STATE TAX_____
(NY, OH & MN residents, please add appropriate local sales tax)

FINAL TOTAL_____
(If paying in Canadian funds, convert using the current exchange rate. UNESCO coupons welcome.)

☐ **BILL ME LATER:** ($5 service charge will be added)
(Bill-me option is good on US/Canada/Mexico orders only; not good to jobbers, wholesalers, or subscription agencies.)

☐ Check here if billing address is different from shipping address and attach purchase order and billing address information.

Signature_____

☐ **PAYMENT ENCLOSED: $**_____

☐ **PLEASE CHARGE TO MY CREDIT CARD.**

☐ Visa   ☐ MasterCard   ☐ AmEx   ☐ Discover
☐ Diners Club
Account #_____

Exp. Date_____

Signature_____

Prices in US dollars and subject to change without notice.

NAME _____

INSTITUTION _____

ADDRESS _____

CITY _____

STATE/ZIP _____

COUNTRY _____ COUNTY (NY residents only) _____

TEL _____ FAX _____

E-MAIL_____
May we use your e-mail address for confirmations and other types of information? ☐ Yes   ☐ No

Order From Your Local Bookstore or Directly From
The Haworth Press, Inc.
10 Alice Street, Binghamton, New York 13904-1580 • USA
TELEPHONE: 1-800-HAWORTH (1-800-429-6784) / Outside US/Canada: (607) 722-5857
FAX: 1-800-895-0582 / Outside US/Canada: (607) 772-6362
E-mail: getinfo@haworthpressinc.com
PLEASE PHOTOCOPY THIS FORM FOR YOUR PERSONAL USE.

BOF96